Changing Painful Patterns
Choosing Healthy Relationships

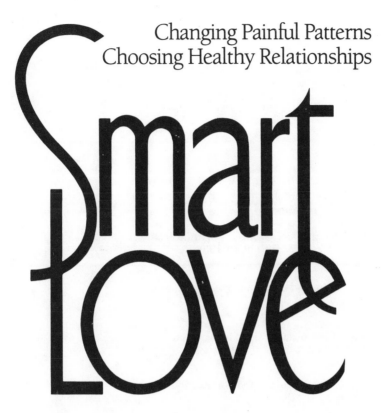

Smart Love

A Codependence Recovery Program
Based on Relationship Addiction Support Groups

JODY HAYES

JEREMY P. TARCHER, INC.
Los Angeles

The Twelve-Steps reprinted and adapted with permission of
Alcoholics Anonymous World Services, Inc.

"How to Start Your Own Support Group" reprinted from
Women Who Love Too Much, copyright © 1985 by Robin
Norwood.

Library of Congress Cataloging-in-Publication Data

Hayes, Jody.
  Smart love : a codependence recovery program based on
  relationship addiction support groups / by Jody Hayes.
    p.   cm.
  ISBN 0-87477-472-1
  1. Relationship addiction. 2. Women—Mental health. I. Title.
RC552.R44H38   1989
158'.24—dc19   88-32451
                                CIP

Jeremy P. Tarcher, Inc.
5858 Wilshire Blvd., Suite 200
Los Angeles, CA 90036

Design by Mike Yazzolino

Manufactured in the United States of America
10 9 8 7 6 5

To Theo, Theodora, Hal, and Steve

"The winter-solstice celebration is far
older than Christianity. It is the
recognition that at the coldest and darkest
times, there is still a core of life deep
within the seeming dead husk, and that life
will push through the old and lifeless
tissue and will flower and bear fruit."
                              Dean G. Watt
                              Family Therapist

Contents

Acknowledgments

I want to acknowledge my debt to Robin Norwood, John Bradshaw, Claudia Black, Sharon Wegscheider-Cruse, Janet Geringer-Woititz, Piero Ferrucci, Howard Halpern, Terence Gorski, Anne Wilson Schaef, Susan Forward, Jacquelyn Small, Melody Beattie, and Stanton Peele, whose important work provided the foundation for this book.

I wish to thank my skilled and caring therapist, Tanya Wilkinson, Ph.D., who nurtured me until I could nurture myself. Many of her ideas and challenging questions appear on the pages that follow. I would also like to thank therapist Rhoda Pregerson for her enthusiasm and the suggestions learned from her practice, as well as therapist Maureen Redl, M.F.C.C., for offering me the benefit of her long experience in working with addictions and for her valuable contributions at the early stages of the book.

Special thanks goes to Theo Gund for inspiring and launching this book. My appreciation goes to therapist and friend Dean G. Watt, Th.M., for allowing me to reproduce in part the message of his 1987 Christmas card as the book's opening quotation.

I am grateful to my loyal friends Theodora Steele, Hal Murphy, Hazel Smith, Vicky Ness, Birgitta Hjalmarson, Doug Shelton, Pamela Bloch, and Joe Walsh for urging me forward, despite formidable obstacles, during the past several years. In the same regard, I'd like to thank Steve McCarthy for his spirited support and Debe and Greg Lefevre for their illuminating contributions.

I am deeply indebted to my editors Connie Zweig and Hank Stine for taking 1,000 intuitive pages and shaping them into a book. This project would not have survived without Hank's skill and support or Peter Beren's persistent enthusiasm. I am grateful to the editorial assistance of Susan Wels, Anne B. McDonald, and Maureen Crist, and to the production and design support of Lynette Padwa.

Each of us has a piece of the truth. I want to acknowledge program friends Suzanne M., Janice G., Patty D., Joan K., Steve O., and Gary C., who gave me permission to turn their ideas into exercises. Always, I felt the support of August O. and Victoria S. across the miles and of Charles R., Christopher D., Jeannie D., and others who allowed me to use their words, which appear as quotations. I am especially grateful to the several dozen courageous women in various cities who allowed me to interview them, many of whose stories appear on these pages. (Identifying details were changed to protect their anonymity.)

I am indebted to the skillful assistance of Kathleen Butler, and to Ellin Donahue, Joan Woodward, Mona Davis, and Martin Stidham for expert word processing. Thanks also goes to Pat Moore for the major task of compiling the national index of groups.

I wish to thank my brothers and sisters Tass, Mimi, Janet, and Phil for their encouragement. I am especially indebted to my brother Buz, who urged me to be open and vulnerable in order to give courage to others. I want to thank my parents, from whom I learned a core sense of values.

Finally, I am grateful for the collective wisdom of all participants in Twelve-Step programs.

Foreword

In 1986 when my book *Men Who Hate Women & the Women Who Love Them* was published, the word *codependence* was not yet in vogue. However, I began at that time to identify the behavior patterns of the partners of troubled men—women who invested their own well-being in fixing their mates. Even then, this message hit home. The book sold more than two million copies.

Today, fortunately, this undefined illness has been fully diagnosed. I, along with other professionals, have explained how many women abdicate their personal dignity and rights in the service of relationships. They deny their own needs and cater to the needs of others. They are plagued by low self-esteem and find their worth in the drama of others' lives. They tend to be on an emotional seesaw, intolerant of differences between people, and unable to say no. Finally, they blame themselves when their mates indulge in addictive sex, drugs, or alcohol.

As a result of the uncovering of this emotional epidemic, *abuse* is no longer defined solely as physical mistreatment. Today abuse has many faces.

Recently there has been a spate of popular books on this topic. Far too many of them, however, describe this painful problem without offering practical solutions. Clearly, not everyone who reads a theoretical book of this kind will go seek help from a psychotherapist. For this reason, support groups for women (and men) who are addicted to unhealthy relationships have become increasingly widespread. They can now be found in every major city.

Some groups follow the tradition of Alcoholics Anonymous' Twelve-Step Program. Others use a less formal peer-group approach. And still others are run by counselors or therapists who specialize in problems with intimacy.

This new book by Jody Hayes is a further sign of hope. It is unique in its workbook format, devoted entirely to tangible how-to's that enable readers to begin to transform the quality of their relationships. *Smart Love* contains a rich variety of tools for changing behavioral patterns: journal writing, fill-in sentences, questionnaires, quizzes, visualization techniques. These are strategies everyone can use, and together they create a strong self-help program.

The book is organized in the logical progression of recovery: from identifying the problem, letting go of obsession, and releasing the past, to nurturing yourself, defining your boundaries, and finding your own brand of spirituality. Each stage builds upon the next, offering wider perspectives and deeper healing. By the end of the workbook, the reader should be able to make more healthy choices about relationship issues and feel a greater capacity for intimacy.

At the end of each chapter, there is a special touch—an inspiring story by a woman who confronted and overcame the obstacles of that stage of recovery. Hopefully, as you work through this book you, too, will find your turning points on the road to recovery.

Smart Love does not attempt to replace individual therapy. It offers support and understanding. It offers a helping hand. But I believe that understanding is only the beginning; without the behavioral changes that result only from committed work, these codependent patterns will remain deeply ingrained.

So be patient with yourself. If an exercise calls for attention to an issue that you have already worked on, look at it more closely this time. If you come up against resistance to a particular subject or to a part of your past, go slowly, respecting your own timing but determining to move ahead.

Smart Love is kind, practical, and hopeful. It shows us the way out of addictive love—and the way in to self-love, which is the beginning of love for another person.

Susan Forward, Ph.D.
March, 1989

Introduction

During the past few years, hundreds of thousands of people across America have been exploring the painful reality of their addiction to love. Both men and women are reading psychologically oriented and personal-growth books on addictive love, watching television talk shows devoted to relationship problems, and forming self-help peer groups to escalate their recovery. Individually and together, these people are creating their own answers to painful problems that once seemed to escape resolution. You may be one of them. Or you may be just beginning your search. In either case, I wrote this book for you.

I am not a therapist or health-care professional. I am simply a woman like you, one who found that her painful patterns in relationships were playing havoc with her life. Fortunately, I found help, and you can, too.

For the last two years, I have been the facilitator of an addictive-love recovery group, where fifty to sixty women meet weekly to explore their difficulties in having healthy love relationships. I know from my own experience, as well as from the experiences of others, that addictive love can cause great unhappiness in one's life. About three years ago, I, too, was trapped in a hopeless relationship. I kept trying harder to please the man in my life, to help him, and to change him into the man of my fantasies. Instead, my relationship became more tense and more hopeless. I thought I was loving. Now I know I was loving too much.

I had read Robin Norwood's *Women Who Love Too Much,*
and although I had never been in love with an alcoholic or a
drug addict, many of the points she made about women in such
relationships were also true for me. I knew the pain of watching
myself make the same mistakes over and over again. I knew the
emptiness she described.

I realized at the time that in order for me to recover from
my problem, I needed to be around other women who felt
trapped by patterns of the past but who wanted very much to
change. I was lucky. I found one of the support groups inspired
by *Women Who Love Too Much* and began attending.

Here were forty women—different in age, interests, and
professional positions—who shared the same deep-rooted dilemma. In childhood, in work, in our adult relationships, we had
automatically placed the needs of others before our own. In
romantic relationships, especially, we had made whatever sacri-
fices we felt were required in order to avoid emotional abandonment. The results in our daily lives had been devastating.

Some of the women in the group had been mentally and
physically abused. Others had devoted years to a series of destructive relationships with men who appeared to be incapable
of intimacy. Others had allowed themselves to become so emotionally dependent on men that they were unable to envision
independent survival. And a few had lost their self-respect to
the degree that they had attempted suicide.

The first afternoon was a turning point. As I told my own
story in vivid detail, I realized I could never go back to my
boyfriend, John, or to my old way of being in relationships
with men.

For a time, I felt enraged with my lover and what he had
done to me. Then I felt enraged with myself and what *I* had
done to me. Soon, that anger gave way to other feelings. I could
see that John and I had lied to each other—and to ourselves—
about who we were, what we wanted, and why we were together. Ultimately, it wasn't just these pretenses that I had to
face, but the carefully assembled pretenses of a lifetime.

For months thereafter, I religiously attended the hour-and-
a-half support-group meeting every Saturday. I heard the same
stories from women who had been married for thirty years and
from women whose longest relationships had lasted three

months; from professional, highly fashionable women and from battered wives who were living in shelters. I really listened to those women. I learned, and I started to heal.

I learned that my extreme "generosity" was not always motivated by noble intentions. Often, I gave to others to gain their approval and acceptance and to boost my self-esteem. I learned that part of my need for privacy and for a sense of self-containment was generated by my poor self-image: I just didn't want anyone to become aware of my typical human flaws. I learned how my unwillingness to let anyone see me as I am had locked out the possibility of genuine intimacy. No one can love someone he doesn't know—and no one knew me. I had made sure of that.

I learned that my overinvolvement in my lover's life, my worrying about his problems and feeling his pain, was not merely due to my sympathetic nature. It was a way for me to avoid getting my own life together, to stop focusing on my own needs and feelings. Loving him too much meant not loving myself enough.

With the help of the group, I made the decision to begin to learn the truth about who I was and why I behaved the way I did. I began to see that personal *discovery* doesn't come from simply understanding concepts about self-healing. Rather, it comes from applying that understanding again and again in one's daily life. Real, lasting *recovery* comes from changing painful patterns and choosing healthy relationships. Once I began to change these deep patterns and make new choices, I began to grow into a woman who could choose to be either intimate with a man or happily on my own.

DEVELOPING THE CAPACITY FOR SMART LOVE

You, too, can make the transition from hurting to healing and to living a better life. This book is designed to help you develop a healthier self, to move from feelings of pain and emptiness to a sense of wholeness. As you read the text and complete the exercises, you should experience a new level of self-awareness about how you think, feel, and behave in intimate relationships.

This is a book about "smart" love, as opposed to addictive love. When love is smart, you get your sense of self-worth from within. When love is addictive, you seek it from the approval of others. When love is smart, you're involved in a pleasurable give and take; when it is addictive, you give until you're empty. When love is smart, you empathize with your lover's feelings; when love is addictive, you become consumed with his feelings and lose touch with your own. When love is smart, you refuse to allow others to abuse or misuse you; when it is addictive, you may become the victim of others' needs.

Smart love is not about finding or forgetting a man. It is about finding and forgiving yourself. There are healthy people involved in intimate relationships, and there are healthy people who are on their own. But before you can make such a choice, you must first choose to be healthy.

This book is for:

- Those in support groups working together toward healthier love relationships. This book can be used in a group setting to enhance the transitions involved in personal change. The exercises can be done before, during, or after meetings. Discussions can be easily structured around the exercise material.

- Those in support groups who prefer to do the exercises privately.

- Those who don't have access to groups or don't wish to attend one. Again, you can use the exercises in this book on your own. They make up a personal program for awareness and recovery that is gentle and profound.

- Those in psychotherapy. It can help focus your insights on relationship issues or help you move out of a "stuck" place.

OTHERS WHO LOVE TOO MUCH

As a support-group facilitator, my experience has been primarily with women's groups; therefore, I have directed this book specifically to women in relationships with men. However, I do not wish to imply that only women are involved in addictive relationships. A man may also engage in obsessive patterns in his romantic relationships, especially if he is from a dysfunctional family.

Addictive love patterns can be seen throughout all types of relationships: women with women, men with men, and parents with children. As you read this book, supply the pronoun appropriate to your particular situation.

The Twelve-Step Process

In this book you will discover much material about relationship-addiction recovery groups. These groups are roughly based on the Twelve-Step groups for recovering alcoholics. As Timmen Cermak, M.D., writes in his book *A Time to Heal:*

> The origin of current self-help programs is the fellowship of Alcoholics Anonymous, which codified the principles of recovery into a series of twelve steps in the mid-1930s. These steps became the backbone of a successful program of recovery that has gradually been recognized to be applicable to a variety of other similar problems. The first were those faced by people who are married to alcoholics (Al-Anon) and by their teenage children (Alateen). Now the programs also address drug abuse (Narcotics Anonymous and Cocaine Anonymous), eating disorders (Overeaters Anonymous), gambling disorders (Gamblers Anonymous), and compulsive spending (Debtors Anonymous). Recently, many adult children of alcoholics have also discovered the value of these same Twelve Steps, and they have been attending self-help meetings in rapidly increasing numbers (either through Al-Anon Adult Children of Alcoholics meetings or the newer ACA fellowships). The Twelve-Step self-help programs work through two avenues: the discipline of working the Twelve Steps, and the personal fellowship of coming together in meetings of the recovering community.
>
> Among the important values reiterated are the need to maintain confidentiality (this is the reason only first names are used); the need for each member to assess what portions of the meeting have personal value (the suggestion that you "take what you like, and leave the rest" is part of what is

repeated at each meeting); and the prohibition against giving advice, criticizing, or analyzing one another ("There will be no cross-talk" is also heard at each meeting).

If you have a chemical dependency, get help in the appropriate Twelve-Step organization (Alcoholics Anonymous, Cocaine Anonymous, or Narcotics Anonymous) before taking on relationship issues. First things must come first.

The Twelve Steps upon which Alcoholics Anonymous and other groups are based have helped hundreds of thousands of people find the inner strength to cope with, and ultimately conquer, their addictions.

HOW THIS BOOK IS ORGANIZED

Smart Love is organized around the stages of recovery from addictive love. Each chapter contains valuable, effective exercises to help you successfully master each new step. These exercises are drawn from a wide range of sources, including my own recovery group, other support groups around the country, therapists I have interviewed, and my reading of the literature. At the end of each chapter you will find a "turning point" story by a woman who has met the challenge of moving through that stage. She tells, in her own words, about her recovery process.

Because these personal explorations are intriguing and may entice you to look further, I have included a section listing resources that you may find helpful. This section is a good resource for the reader who wants to further explore any of the particular stages of recovery. You will also find a national directory of support groups at the back of the book.

The material is presented in an "emotionally chronological" order, a sequence that will most likely mirror your own inner experience of the work. The exercises naturally flow into one another, and this rhythm can help to keep you moving through the book.

Chapter 1 discusses addictive love and its source in codependence, as well as the childhood forces that can create these patterns.

Chapter 2 discusses the possibility of recovery from addictive love and lets you know what resources you can draw on to help you begin.

Chapter 3 discusses the first stage of letting go of your overinvolvement in the lives of others.

Chapter 4 focuses on learning to love and nurture yourself. It looks at the ways in which you may have unwittingly prevented this from happening and offers exercises to help you develop a clear sense of self-worth.

Chapter 5 focuses on releasing the past. The exercises are designed to help you take a closer look at childhood rules that may influence your relationships today.

Chapter 6 is directed toward recovery of a stronger sense of self.

Chapter 7 is about building stronger boundaries between yourself and others, a necessary component of healthy relationships.

Chapter 8 looks at the possibility of developing a sense of the spiritual in your life.

Chapter 9 explores options. It will help you become more aware not only of important decisions in relationships but also of the small, everyday choices that affect the way you live.

Chapter 10 suggests ways in which you can increase your capacity for healthy intimacy with family, friends, and lovers. Empathy, sharing, and compatibility are some of the topics included here.

HOW TO USE THIS BOOK

Smart Love is a sourcebook that presents a program of exercises and ideas for personal growth and development. You may want to purchase a notebook or journal in which you can preserve your insights and discoveries without being limited by the writing space provided in this book.

In answering the questions raised by the exercises, it is very important that you actually write your answers down on paper (being sure to date each page) and then that you reread them as you work through the book. At a later date in your recovery, you may want to respond again to these questions in order to discover how your answers have changed. Rereading your earlier answers will help you to see the changes in your attitudes, beliefs, and feelings over time. Too, it will give you a sense of the complexities of relationship addiction and of why it is so difficult to resolve problems so that they stay resolved.

When using a separate binder, write out each question as it appears in this book before writing your answer. Writing the questions helps you to get started and to focus your attention on the fact that it is *you* who is being asked to respond. When you are asked to complete a sentence, or when you are asked a direct question, there is no pretending that this is somebody's else's problem.

Sometimes, in these exercises, several possible answers are given (for instance, "I feel angry, excited, frustrated, relieved"). These are only examples. If you come up with a word that is more appropriate for you, then that is the best word for you to use.

Do not feel obligated to complete every exercise. However, if you find yourself avoiding a particular exercise or chapter, take a good look at your resistance and then make a special effort to work in that area of the book. This may be precisely the chapter or exercise that can really begin to help you heal.

Write out your answers fully—that is, don't use just a word or short phrase, but write complete sentences and paragraphs. You will find that the process of writing, in and of itself, will draw you deeper and deeper into your psychological processes, helping you to gain awareness and perspectives that you may not have known you had. You may also find yourself gaining insight into a whole range of problems and possibilities that are not touched on by this book. As you reach new points of awareness, you might want to discuss this with your support group or therapist.

You may be surprised from time to time at the power of the feelings that rise to the surface as you do these exercises. You may wish to cry or scream or simply give up. At times you may feel such sadness or loss that you may feel paralyzed.

At those moments, remember this: let yourself feel the feelings as fully as you can. Don't try to push yourself to finish an exercise; don't try to think your way out of an emotion.

Simply let yourself be. You will find that, slowly and naturally, you will come out the other side, ready at a future time to pick up the book again.

Giving yourself permission to feel your feelings is a key to recovery. Denying your feelings will only slow down the recovery process; acknowledging them will speed it up—and bring healing. Emotional healing is at the heart of personal change.

AS YOU BEGIN . . .

The recovery program described in this book will start you on your journey of self-exploration. This book does not presume to provide answers to all of your questions about addictive love or solutions to all of your dilemmas about relationships. No book can replace a good therapist or support group.

For example, this book will not:

- solve all your problems
- remove the discomfort that accompanies any change
- compel you to do anything you are not ready for
- tell you how or where to find a romantic partner
- help you pretend that "everything is fine"
- help you pretend that problems will just fade away without involvement on your part

However, this book may:

- help you to better understand your motivations
- help you to realize you are not alone in your quest for better relationships
- help you to discover new strengths within yourself
- help you to let go of control, fear, and anxiety
- encourage you to finally take action to improve your life, including getting professional help should you want it
- help you to better understand your loved ones and why they do what they do

- help you begin to forgive yourself and others
- help reduce the incidence of depression by helping you to clarify and express your feelings
- help you rediscover some spiritual aspect of your nature
- help you discover new, positive aspects to your life
- help you break destructive patterns and choose healthier friends and lovers
- demystify what constitutes a healthy or an unhealthy relationship
- learn new relationship skills
- provide you with models for satisfying intimacy
- help you to improve the quality of all your relationships, romantic and otherwise

At the least, *Smart Love* can set you off in the right direction and give you the tools you need to stay on the path. Furthermore, it may help you to break out of a "holding pattern" in your recovery, to deal with those times when you feel as if you are not making progress. It will offer you insights and a heightened self-awareness concerning painful patterns in your relationships.

If you use this book wisely, move through it thoughtfully, and return to it as if to a good friend, you will be well on your way to developing *smart love.*

Moving Beyond
Addictive Relationships

" " I know I'm in trouble when I turn to something or someone outside of myself to make me happy. **" "**

COLLEEN

Why are we irresistibly drawn to certain men? Why do some of us stay in unfulfilling relationships long after we recognize that the negative far outweighs the positive? And why do we feel unable to leave these relationships?

As many of us know from personal experience, there is a certain level of excitement in an unfulfilling romance—a state of bliss mixed with a sense of despair—that is simply not present in a healthier relationship. We may actually become "hooked" on this form of excitement and mistake it for love. But if we have grown accustomed to fears about our lover's leaving, or fears about what he will do next, then perhaps we have confused love with obsession.

Some psychologists compare the intoxicating yet painful "altered state" of an obsessive relationship to the "high" produced by a drug. At first it may seem odd to consider parallels between characteristics of the more obvious forms of addiction, such as alcoholism or cocaine addiction, and the less obvious addictive characteristics that can appear in personal relationships. Yet the names of three very popular perfumes—Opium, Obsession, and Poison—offer clues to the addictive, obsessive, and even destructive nature of much of the "love" we see and experience. Robin Norwood, the author of *Women Who Love Too Much*, considers relationship addiction "the most romanticized addiction of all."

ARE YOU ADDICTED TO RELATIONSHIPS?

The following quiz can help you to identify whether you are addicted to unhealthy relationships. Your willingness to take this quiz indicates your desire to look at yourself honestly. It means you have the courage needed to work toward a new, more satisfying way to love. Your clear, precise identification of the problem is the first step toward your recovery.

Answer each of these questions "T" or "F" for True or False.

_____ You often feel magnetically drawn to someone. You act on this feeling even when you suspect that this person or the relationship may not be good for you.

_____ When you are not in a relationship, you feel depressed. Meeting a new man usually cures your feelings of depression and boosts your self-esteem.

_____ When you consider breaking up with a man, you worry about what will happen to him without you.

_____ To avoid being alone following a breakup, you immediately start to look for a new man.

_____ Despite exerting intelligence and independence in other areas, you are distrustful and fearful of independence within a love relationship.

_____ To be happy, you need to have a man in your life.

_____ Even when a relationship isn't good for you, you find it difficult to break up.

_____ You have often been involved with someone who is in some way unavailable. He may live far away, he may be married, he may already be deeply involved with someone else, or he may be emotionally distant.

_____ If a kind, available man likes you, you will probably find him boring and ultimately reject him.

_____ You often "make over" your boyfriend, trying to change him to meet your ideal.

_____ It is hard for you to say no to a man with whom you are involved, whether he wants time, money, sex, or something else.

_____ You do not really believe you deserve a good relationship.

_____ Sexually, you are more concerned with pleasing your partner than with pleasing yourself.

_____ You are unable to stop seeing a certain person even though you know that continuing to see him is destructive to you.

_____ You remain obsessed by the memories of a relationship for months or even years after it has ended.

If you answered True to most of these questions, then you very probably have a long-standing problem with addictive love. Any sentence answered in this way points to an area you may want to work on. But do not lose hope. Recovery is possible, and with it, the opportunity for healthier, nonaddictive relationships in the future.

SYMPTOMS OF ADDICTIVE LOVE

> " Loving too much . . . means, in truth, obsessing about a man and calling that obsession 'love,' allowing it to control your emotions and much of your behavior. . . . It means measuring the degree of your 'love' by the depth of your torment. "
>
> ROBIN NORWOOD

Healthy relationships bear little resemblance to addictive relationships. For example, those who practice smart love *like* the people with whom they are involved. By contrast, it is not uncommon to dislike the person to whom you are addicted. In her support group, Simone says of her six-year relationship, "I couldn't stand this man, but I was totally attached to him."

At other times, the woman does not dislike her lover, but she dislikes *herself* while she is in such a relationship. Love, instead of making one feel good about oneself, has the opposite effect. Monica says, "Jack is my life. I eat, breathe, *live* for this man. He is all I think or talk about." She adds, "This happens every time I fall in love. I get really down on myself for acting like this, but it still goes on."

Often, the addictive relationship heats up quickly, and sex becomes the primary focus. Because the physical intimacy is premature, emotional intimacy has little chance to grow. And the people involved don't stop to question what their deeper connection is about. Says P. J., a college professor and member of a women's recovery group, "I met Rigo at a party and took him home with me. We spent the next two days in bed. After those two days, he asked me to live with him. I thought I was the luckiest person in the world."

P. J. sums up her three-month relationship in this way: "We were wonderful in the bedroom, and we were wonderful in the kitchen, but we were terrible in the living room. We couldn't talk to each other. We had nothing in common, and I really knew it from the start."

Los Angeles therapist Rhoda Pregerson describes still another addictive pattern: The woman is afraid to open up sexually until the man says "I love you." After they make love, she falls for him quickly and begins to become obsessed—while he pulls back from her clinging. Typically, she struggles to please in an effort to reel him in so that she can feel safe. Meanwhile, he struggles to get free in an effort to avoid feeling smothered. It's a dance that can last for years.

Although two-week romances and three-month relationships are common lengths of involvement, other women are involved in thirty-year marriages or ten-year affairs in which they find little satisfaction—and which they cannot leave. Something in the dynamic of the relationship entraps them.

Many intelligent and otherwise independent women get caught up in relationships with men who are not good for them. Although some women break loose quickly, others stay in these destructive involvements long after they first recognize that the negative far outweighs the positive. They get stuck, too paralyzed by their addictive love to do anything about the situation—including seeking outside help. Furthermore, if the relationship falls apart, many of these women will accept 100 percent of the blame for what went wrong.

Some women feel too embarrassed to talk to their friends about this problem. Instead, they pretend everything is all right. Like a person addicted to a substance, a woman in such a situation treats her relationship problems with secrecy and hides her troubles.

Others have talked compulsively about this problem for so long to so many different people that they may feel they have "used up" their friends and can no longer turn to them. Either way, these women feel isolated—which only adds to their sense of paralysis and despair.

RECOGNIZING THE PATTERN OF ADDICTIVE LOVE

What is a relationship addiction like? What does it feel like?

The following is a summary of the relationship-addiction process, as described by San Francisco therapist Susan Peabody in her booklet *Addiction to Love:*

1. The woman experiences a powerful attraction to another person.

2. An infatuation (the idealizing of someone she does not know very well) develops.

3. Romantic love blossoms, and the addiction is triggered.

4. The woman projects onto the loved one her dreams for eternal happiness.

5. A compulsive preoccupation with the loved one develops.

6. The woman embraces the illusion that only this particular person can make her happy or satisfy her desire to love and be loved.

7. Dependence takes root. A sense of "choice" disappears as options narrow concerning how the woman will spend her time, how she sees herself, and whom she is able to love.

8. The woman begins to demonstrate obsessive behavior. She waits for her lover to call; she loses track of her friends; her work life suffers; and she allows herself to be mistreated.

9. The relationship begins to deteriorate under the stress of her obsession.

10. The woman's physical and emotional well-being begins to deteriorate.

11. If the relationship continues, she may develop minor health problems or a serious illness.

12. If the relationship ends, another addictive relationship begins.

CODEPENDENCE

“A codependent person is one who has let another person's behavior affect him or her, and who is obsessed with controlling that person's behavior.”

MELODY BEATTIE

We have been discussing addictive, obsessive love—what Robin Norwood has called "loving too much." While addictive love and loving too much denote how a woman relates to a romantic partner, *codependence* is the term used to describe how she interacts in all her relationships, romantic and otherwise.

The codependent seeks approval from practically everyone with whom she comes into contact. Instead of building a life around one person, she may have several "golden calves" around whom she dances—perhaps her mother and father, her women friends, her boss, and the clerk at the supermarket, in addition to her lover. She lives her life around the needs of others.

Where there is addictive love, there is often another form of substance abuse as well. Perhaps the woman's lover is addicted to alcohol, cocaine, or marijuana. In such instances a parallel develops: the alcoholic is obsessed with his alcohol, and the woman is obsessed with him. Sometimes the woman's partner is not substance addicted but is addicted to work, money, or sex. The resulting relationship pattern is the same.

The woman may also be substance addicted, but when she is actively "loving too much" she often becomes more worried about her lover's addictive behavior than about her own. When two people have addictive personalities, they can easily become addicted to each other.

Addiction robs us of our wholeness. It makes us feel as though we are less than complete as human beings. We must then quickly find our "other half"—another half-person with whom we can become enmeshed. In this case, unfortunately, two halves do not make a whole.

The common denominator in addictive relationships is not the length of the relationship, whether or not the couple is married, or even whether there is any genuine caring. The common denominator seems to be a progressive behavior pattern that leads to what is called codependence.

In the language of substance abuse, the term *codependent* (or enabler) is typically used to describe the person who unwittingly encourages the alcoholic and enables him to continue his addiction. This term has come to be more widely used today to describe the tendency of many individuals to live their lives by, for, and in reaction to another person—or to the world at large.

Sowing the Seeds for Codependence

Often, codependent behavior begins in families in which substance abuse or some other dysfunction, such as physical or emotional abuse, exists. The growing child is forced to live her life around the alcoholic or abusive adult's needs and to ignore her own needs. To survive, she learns to be a "good girl." She takes on the role of rescuing others.

Many women in addictive relationships come from dysfunctional families. There is little nurturing in such homes; Robin Norwood says that family problems, often with alcohol or other drugs, prevent a child from receiving needed lessons on how to love and be nurtured: "The woman, as she grows older, tries to fill this unmet need vicariously by becoming a caregiver, especially to men who appear in some way needy."

Alcohol or other drugs need not be present for this pattern to emerge. Nebraska psychotherapist Mij Laging says that

> a dysfunctional family can exist at a variety of levels. Characteristics include spouse or child abuse; constant arguing or tension; compulsive behavior such as gambling, eating or working; inappropriate sexual behavior on the part of a parent toward a child; and extreme rigidity about or obsession with money.

Dysfunction can also exist in a family in which there is little genuine communication or tolerance for the feelings of individual family members. Mental illness in a parent or child can also produce dysfunction in the family. Says Laging, "The woman from a dysfunctional family will try harder to make a relationship work in order to right the wrongs of past family relationships that did not succeed."

Typically, it is not as if the members of a dysfunctional family are actually withholding love. More often, they just don't know how to love in healthy ways.

Unfortunately, the dysfunctional family is more the rule than the exception. According to psychologist Terence Gorski, a functional family is one that teaches a child to "relate in a productive manner with other human beings." Using this definition, Gorski estimates that only 20 to 30 percent of adults in the United States come from functional families.

Addictive love and the codependent behavior behind it can make us very unhappy. It sets us up for lives of pain and loss. Yet, codependence is extremely common—Houston therapist John Bradshaw calls it "the addiction most in need of treatment."

A Society of Codependents

Even if you come from a healthy, loving family, you still may have had a hard time resisting our culture's bias toward viewing women as caretakers and nurturers. Radio, television, and books send the same message in a continuing barrage: a woman's primary role in life is to nurture others.

Not long ago, the only acceptable occupations for women were as nurturers—for example, as teachers, nurses, or mothers. Even today, most girls are taught by their families to take care of others first. Our culture seconds that view. Scan a supermarket magazine rack or the romance section of a bookstore, look at television and movie role models, or listen to the words to current popular songs, and you'll get the same message: you are nothing without a man. Although our attitude about women's careers has changed somewhat in recent years, women are still openly encouraged to be nurturers of the family and the world. Nurturing others is a very positive trait, but not when we take on that role to the neglect of ourselves.

Much as we would like to, we cannot quickly and radically reverse the prevailing tide of culture. Therapist Ginny NiCarthy, in her book *Getting Free,* writes that "all people in Western civilization have been taught to be addicted to romantic love, but women, especially, are socialized to believe they are only half a person without an intimate partner." While women can work collectively on cultural change, we can pay even more effective attention to our own lives.

By seeing patterns in your life that have been painful to you and changing those patterns with the help of this and other books and a support group, you will be improving your life—and in so doing, improving the culture at large.

Are You a Codependent?

Codependence affects people in many ways. Among its symptoms are low self-esteem, obsession with others, inability to trust, confused emotions, weak personal boundaries, compulsive caretaking, constant denial of the problems caused by codependence, and difficulty with sexual issues.

The following checklist will help you to review the problems associated with codependence. Read each of the statements below and put a check mark next to the ones that are true for you. If many of these statements describe your behavior, then you may be a codependent. Read through the list a second time and put a second check mark next to any area that feels particularly important or troublesome to you. There are chapters in this book that apply especially to some areas.

Self-Esteem

_____   I come from a perfect family.

_____   I come from a dysfunctional family.

_____   I tend to blame myself for everything that goes wrong.

_____   I fear rejection.

_____   I fear anger in myself.

_____   I am frightened by an angry voice.

_____   I expect myself to do everything perfectly.

_____   I take criticism personally.

_____   I feel different from other people.

_____   I am constantly looking for approval.

Obsession with Others

_____   I notice the flaws in others.

_____   I shouldn't feel so tired.

_____   I talk about other people much of the time.

_____   I lose sleep worrying.

_____   I consider image and appearance very important.

Inability to Trust Rationally

_____   I feel unsure of my decisions.

_____   I trust people I don't really know.

_____   I don't trust other people.

_____   I lose faith in myself every time I make a small mistake.

_____   I adopt the point of view of my partner.

Confused Emotions

_____ I feel resentful that I'm responsible for so many others.

_____ I laugh when I feel like crying.

_____ I find it difficult to be spontaneous.

_____ I sometimes feel like a martyr because I sacrifice so much.

_____ I feel guilty much of the time.

Weak Personal Boundaries

_____ I complain about what he is doing but stay with him anyway.

_____ I can be completely intolerant.

_____ I tolerate anything.

_____ I say no, yet still do what is asked of me.

_____ If someone abuses me verbally, I will probably stand there and take it.

_____ I can be critical of others' personal habits.

_____ I get embarrassed when other people make mistakes.

Caretaking

_____ I feel safer when giving rather than receiving.

_____ I am "on call" to friends with problems at any hour of the day or night.

_____ I feel responsible for other people's thoughts, feelings, choices, well-being, health, and destiny.

_____ I try to please other people instead of myself.

_____ I see other people as the source of my problems.

_____ I am attracted to needy people, especially men.

_____ I feel compelled to solve other people's problems.

_____ I know what other people need, want, and should do.

_____ I take care of other people by fixing their flaws for them.

_____ I feel unappreciated much of the time.

_____ I often give unsolicited advice.

_____ I need drama and excitement in my life.

_____ I grow resentful when others are not willing to "give" like I do.

Denial

_____ I ignore how I am feeling.

_____ I refuse to pay attention to negative feelings.

_____ I pretend things are better than they are.

_____ I spend money compulsively.

_____ I watch my problems get worse.

_____ I want to believe other people's lies.

_____ I would tell a lie to protect a friend's feelings.

_____ I would tell a lie to keep a situation from getting out of hand.

_____ I sometimes lie to myself.

_____ I stay busy so I won't have to think about important matters.

Sexuality

_____ I cater to his needs at the expense of my own.

_____ I let just about anyone hug me.

_____ I engage in sex when I don't want to.

_____ I find it difficult or embarrassing to ask for what would please me sexually.

_____ I pretend I am aroused when I am not.

_____ I do things sexually that I don't enjoy.

The next section will help you to better understand what causes you to stay stuck in codependent behavior.

Reinforcing Codependence

Codependence is reinforced when you unconsciously bombard your mind with negative messages, such as "You'll never be good enough" or "You don't deserve better." Some of these messages were learned in childhood, others are culturally induced. Many of them contain enough truth so that they seem to be a description of an enduring and inescapable reality. They are, however, only partial descriptions of your past and incomplete descriptions of your potential. At this point it will be helpful to review some of the self-talk with which you destroy your ability to function well on your own behalf.

"I'm a loser in love."   Many women who are codependent feel that they are losers in love because the relationships they have formed have not worked out. Indeed, in past relationships you may have unknowingly fallen into destructive patterns. But during your recovery process, you will unlearn old, destructive patterns and learn new skills about relationships. As your relationships begin to work, you will develop a more positive self-image.

"If I were really okay, I'd be in a relationship."   Actually, being okay or healthy has nothing to do with being in or out of a romantic relationship. You can be very healthy and yet currently free of a romantic relationship. You can be unhealthy and involved in one.

"He's not the man I want, but I can change him."   When you feel you don't deserve better, you will tend to accept unsatisfying relationships. There's a direct connection between your level of self-esteem and your choice of men. Also, when you appreciate yourself, it's much easier for another person to appreciate you.

"If he would only stop _____ (drinking, getting high, having affairs, being verbally abusive), we would be happy."   When you live according to an "If only he . . ." statement, you define your happiness as dependent on another person's changing. His problem becomes your problem; you lose yourself in him. This is a deadly pattern—one that needs breaking.

"I can't believe I did that. I must be crazy."   During and after an addictive relationship, many very sane individuals feel as though they have lost control and are going mad. Seeing your patterns for the first time can be a rude awakening.

If you are recently coming out of an addictive relationship, or if you are looking at a history of pain and loss in past relationships, you may be feeling pain, grief, or rage. The intensity of your feelings may seem frightening. But you are not going crazy. Whatever you are feeling, let those honest feelings surface. Allowing yourself to feel them is a sign of mental health.

"I can't change."   Most women involved in destructive relationships feel helpless to alter their patterns. They have tried to kick the addictive love habits in the past but have been unsuccessful. Perhaps they weren't really ready, or perhaps they didn't have the necessary tools. However, many people just like you successfully recover from love addiction to lead more satisfying and fulfilling lives, even after histories of prior failures. Your time, too, may well be now.

Breaking the Cycle

There is hope. You *can* break the cycle. This painful pattern is not your essence, but something you have learned and can therefore unlearn. The turning point toward recovery at this stage comes when you realize that you can break the pattern of constantly choosing destructive or obsessive relationships. Society encouraged this behavioral pattern, and you unwittingly went along with it.

When you see that addictive love is not a disease but an imbalance, you will understand that changing does not mean giving up any essential part of yourself. It is simply a matter of striking the right balance.

You can love without giving yourself away. You can care without being a martyr. You can make peace with love.

The irony of relationship addiction is that it damages many of our best qualities and makes them work against us. Our involvement in obsessive relationships demonstrates (although in a frightfully out-of-balance way) our enormous capacity for giving, loving, caring, nurturing, and understanding.

As you progress through this book, you will redirect your energy toward people and activities that will nourish you in new, healthy ways. Because your life has been so outer-directed, you must first take an inner journey in order to see your own strength. Once you have a stronger sense of self, you will be able to attract and appreciate healthier individuals and enjoy a broader spectrum of experiences. Instead of being preoccupied by destructive romance, you will find friends of both sexes who stimulate and replenish you.

For a time, the only difference in your situation may be in your approach to decision making. Though your options about how to spend your time and with whom to spend it may seem new and varied, it is likely that these options have been there all along. You will see that in every situation there are several choices open to you. You may still, at times, place someone else's needs before your own. But now you will be making a conscious choice, not following a compulsion. Your newfound ability to recognize and take action on healthy options is a sure step on the road to emotional healing.

As you continue on your journey, keep in mind the traveler who walks two steps forward and one step back. Unexpected obstacles will surely present themselves; mistakes and setbacks are inevitable. But by placing yourself in a healing environment and feeling support from others, you will be able to overcome these obstacles and move forward. The pace of your renewal is not the main point. Your commitment to recovery is. Expect old habits to return from time to time; when they do, be gentle with yourself. Remember, it is what you do with these habits that is important.

Your problems won't vanish overnight, of course. But as you recover, the changes in how you see yourself and others will start to affect the people and events around you in new and exciting ways. Being on the road to recovery means discovering your real self, perhaps for the first time.

If you feel "stuck" at any point along the way, you may want to stop and do something different. Put the book down. Take a walk. Pick some flowers. Meditate. Then come back to the book and do an exercise or read any woman's story that appeals to you.

Your Path to Recovery

&&I had heard of group support, but I had never actually experienced it until I walked through that door.??

SIMONE

Recovery begins when you commit to changing your attitudes and your behavior. First, you have to be willing to admit that there is a problem—addictive love. Then, you have to be willing to *do* something about it, to make new priorities in your relationships and in your life as a whole.

It takes humility to admit that sometimes we don't have all the answers. This may be difficult for those of us who have prided ourselves on our absolute independence. We might want to think about another tough time when we reached out for help—and were thankful that someone was there for us. Now we will make many new friends who will also be there for us. With a receptive mind, we are ready for the new path that is open to us.

Whatever our reasons for starting to take action, we will not be alone on this journey. It is a highly unusual person who can recover from obsessive relationship patterns totally on her own. Most of us need the support of friends, peers, and professionals in order to heal. That is why support groups are the most popular method for women seeking to recover from relationship addiction. Since every person in the room knows exactly how the others feel, they can all give one another the understanding they need. This chapter focuses on getting you the support and encouragement you will very likely need.

Every journey starts with a first step. No matter what that first step is, it is a crucial one.

ONE SMALL STEP

When you take that first step in the right direction, you will feel better about yourself. You will also be on your way to a more satisfying life and more satisfying relationships.

Your very first step will probably be a small one. You might decide not to call your lover today or not to criticize your husband. If that is too difficult, see if you can avoid the action for half a day—perhaps the afternoon.

Other suggestions for small first steps: Do any exercise in this book that interests you. Pick one of the first-person accounts of recovery that you can best relate to and picture yourself as that person, accomplishing your own goals for growth. If you have been thinking about going to a therapist and have been given a recommendation for one, call to make an appointment. If you have no recommendation, ask friends for names and then follow up with a call. If you have been considering attending some type of support group, call for a meeting schedule or pick a night to go to one. Write the date down on your calendar.

Any appropriate step you take, no matter how small, will help you to feel better. After all, recovery is not a single giant leap into the unknown, but a gradual process of taking small steps until you have traveled a surprising distance and begun to build a foundation for your new life.

If you are having difficulty finding a step small enough to take because they all seem overwhelming, don't become angry with yourself. Break any of these actions into smaller pieces until you are able to do one positive thing on your own behalf. For example, instead of trying to read this entire book in a weekend, do one exercise or read one story at a time. If you have recently broken up with someone, instead of saying, "I'll never see him again," decide to spend three days without seeing him. With each small step, you will begin to regain a sense of power in your choices and an ability to take care of yourself.

MARSHALING A SUPPORT NETWORK

> "I don't need everybody in the world to approve my recovery. I only need one or two people who will say, 'Good going, you did it!'"
>
> MONICA

As you begin to master taking small steps, it may be important for you to break the silence with which you have surrounded your destructive relationships. Have you stopped calling old friends because you have spent so much time with your man? Have you stayed off the phone altogether, hoping he will call you? When was the last time you went out with a group of women or a male friend who is not a lover or potential lover? Have you broken engagements with family or friends on short notice to cater to one of your lover's whims? If so, perhaps you have been unintentionally isolating yourself.

If you have one or two close friends, this is the time to tell them about how you are feeling about your relationship problems. Find one or more people you can trust. Go slowly, revealing only a little information at a time to see whether they react out of loving concern rather than disapproval.

If a friend responds in a way that feels good to you, tell her that this is a difficult time and ask if you can call her again in a few days. If discussing issues on the telephone makes you uncomfortable, you might prefer to meet in person.

Howard M. Halpern, author of *How to Break Your Addiction to a Person,* says that the formation of a support network should not be left to chance. However, he continues, forming such a network requires the ability to trust. If you are not accustomed to trusting, it may be particularly difficult to do this at a time when you are vulnerable.

> If you do not have many or any friends to take this risk with, that fact is probably telling you much about why you became

addicted in the first place—that you put too many of your needs into this one relationship for lack of other relationships. It may also be saying that your addiction to that one relationship narrowed your world so much that there are now not enough other connections.

Halpern says that a time of crisis in your relationship can work to your benefit: "You can use the crisis in your life to motivate you to take a risk." That risk can involve looking closely at the people in your life to see who supports your efforts to change and who gets in your way.

Snipers and Supporters

To your dismay, you may find that some of your longtime friends and members of your family may not support your new attitude and actions. If you tell a certain friend that you're not seeing your man as often, she may think you are going to be critical of *her* relationship. She may feel threatened by the implications of what you are doing and try to pull you back into your old routine.

Families are often resistant because if one member changes, other members' roles often change as well. For instance, if you decide to avoid romantic entanglements for a while, your mother may feel she has failed in her role because having a successful relationship is her measure of success as a woman.

For this reason, you may want to avoid people or situations that threaten to sabotage your recovery until you feel more stable and self-confident. You can identify these people and behaviors through the exercise below. (If you've purchased a notebook, as suggested in the Introduction, you may wish to use it when completing this exercise and those throughout the rest of the book.)

Snipers.   Snipers are people who undermine your efforts to break unhealthy relationship patterns. They may tell you that you are selfish for wanting more from a relationship, or they may imply that you should be rescuing your lover from his problems. They may blame you for his alcohol or substance abuse. They may contact your lover and encourage him to contact you.

Write down three other sniping behaviors that you have seen or experienced.

1. _____

2. _____

3. _____

Supporters.   Supporters respect your desire to change and when possible are available to talk to you. They do not judge your choices or interfere with your relationships. They encourage you to attend support groups or therapy sessions and to develop creative new options. They demonstrate, through their words and actions, that they want what is best for you.

Now write down three other supportive behaviors that you have experienced.

1. _____

2. _____

3. _____

Don't be surprised if you realize during this exercise that some of your closest "friends" are snipers. If you suspect that someone you love does not support your recovery, you can stop denying this now.

Write in the names of three people you suspect probably do not support your recovery. Briefly describe why you feel this way, giving a specific example.

1. _____

2. _____

3. _____

List here the names and phone numbers of three people who
do support your recovery:

1. _____

2. _____

3. _____

You may feel some relief after clarifying the roles of these
friends or family members. If you still feel uncertain, ask them
more directly how they feel, explaining why you want to know.

Notice how they respond. If your suspicion is confirmed in
any instance, it may be time to take a break from that relationship until you are further along in your recovery.

By identifying potential supporters, you will know who to
turn to in a crisis and with whom to deepen your bonds during
your recovery.

Sometimes you will find that when a friend is allowed to
know why change is so important to you, she may move from
the "sniper" list to your corps of supporters.

Seeking Group Support

If you do not feel comfortable turning to friends, or if your
friendship network is not strong enough to sustain you in difficult times, there are other places to turn—support groups
comprised of women who feel just as you do, who have experienced similar pain, and who are now working toward having a
better life.

Why are support groups so successful? In part, this is so
because many women often find it easier to discuss intimate
issues in the company of people who have not known them for
years and who share similar problems and feelings.

Not every group and not every meeting of any group will
be right for you. But you will know that you are in the right
place when you feel the click of recognition as you listen to
others talk frankly about their feelings. You will know that you
are not alone in facing your problem.

Sharing and Honesty.   Once you are in the right group, you will feel safe, but you may also feel shy. This brings us to another paradox of recovery: the more you reveal yourself, the safer you will feel. The more vulnerable you make yourself, the quicker you can recover.

Share your experience with members of your support group, a good friend, or a therapist. Your problems will become clearer when you give words to them. You will discover how much harder it is to fool yourself when you actually hear yourself saying something that you know is either a partial truth or a full lie. At the same time, when you are describing signs of progress or small victories, you will find their effect amplified when you applaud yourself in the presence of others.

There are some important things to remember about sharing. It is most helpful if you acknowledge how you feel at the moment, whatever those feelings are. Remember, you are not speaking to please others or to be graded on your recovery. You are speaking to help yourself.

Embrace your feelings and accept them, even if you feel momentarily miserable. By honestly describing your feelings, you will get a clearer understanding of the experience you are going through. Moreover, there is a significant chance that your painful feelings will diminish. A side benefit is that you will almost always help someone else who is not yet brave enough to speak.

When speaking, it is important to avoid long, detailed descriptions of what others have done to you, the facts of a given circumstance, the obsessive details. This will only feed your problem, not release you from it. Keep the focus on how you feel, how events affected you, and what you're doing about it.

Finally, when sharing publicly, avoid comparing yourself with others. It is a very natural tendency to believe that you are not doing as well as some other women in your group, especially some who may have been working on their recoveries for longer periods. Their development is not for you to judge; it is totally irrelevant to yours. Keep your focus on yourself.

Choosing a Support Group.   Following is an overview of some of the groups available to those seeking recovery from relationship addiction. These are often called Twelve-Step programs because they use the Twelve Steps to Recovery of Alcoholics Anonymous, the successful organization that helps people to recover from alcoholism.

For those who may be unfamiliar with the premise of these programs, here are the Twelve Steps on which they are modeled:

The Twelve Steps*

1. We admitted we were powerless over alcohol [for our purposes here, we can substitute the word *relationships*]—that our lives had become unmanageable.

2. Came to believe that a Power greater than ourselves could restore us to sanity.

3. Made a decision to turn our will and our lives over to the care of God *as we understood Him.*

4. Made a searching and fearless moral inventory of ourselves.

5. Admitted to God, to ourselves, and to another human being the exact nature of our wrongs.

6. Were entirely ready to have God remove all these defects of character.

7. Humbly asked Him to remove our shortcomings.

8. Made a list of all persons we had harmed and became willing to make amends to them all.

9. Made direct amends to such people wherever possible except when to do so would injure them or others.

10. Continued to take personal inventory, and when we were wrong, promptly admitted it.

11. Sought through prayer and meditation to improve our conscious contact with God *as we understood Him,* praying only for knowledge of His will for us and the power to carry that out.

*The Twelve Steps reprinted for adaptation with permission of Alcoholics Anonymous World Services, Inc.

12. Having had a spiritual awakening as the result of these Steps, we tried to carry this message to others and to practice these principles in all our affairs.

These groups charge no dues, and all have helpful literature that is free for the taking. They also have traditions of anonymity, which means that those attending don't have to give their last names or otherwise reveal themselves to the group.

The Twelve-Step groups are careful to insist that people who attend withhold criticism and judgment. This helps create a psychologically safe environment in which members can reveal their deepest feelings without fear of having them misunderstood or abused.

A final benefit of having a strong support group is the discovery of healthy role models (women further along in their recovery), from whom you can gain insight about the road ahead and its pitfalls and high peaks. In time, you will find yourself—perhaps to your surprise—as a role model for other women.

Most of these programs recommend that you attend six meetings in as short a time as possible to get the full taste of how the programs work. In fact, the turning point at this stage of recovery comes when you can make this commitment. While there are many types of recovery groups, you may want to attend a group that focuses solely on the study of the Twelve Steps in order for you to gain a faster understanding of the steps' special ability to help you.

Al-Anon. As mentioned earlier, psychologists now believe that a large number of relationship addicted women come from families that were dysfunctional because of alcohol or other drug use. Al-Anon, the counterpart to Alcoholics Anonymous, is designed for the families and friends of alcoholics. I would suggest beginning your search for a support network there.

Al-Anon is an excellent place to learn how to put the focus on yourself instead of on the problem person in your life. Because its network is so well established, there is most likely an Al-Anon group in your community.

There are also special Al-Anon groups for Adult Children of Alcoholics (ACoA or CoA) groups.

Adult Children of Alcoholics Groups.   Adult Children of Alcoholics (ACA) is a relatively new organization, created to assist people in releasing and parenting the inner child.

(Al-Anon/ACoA and ACA are independent but mutually cooperative organizations. Listings for each may be found in the white pages of your telephone directory. Groups may call themselves what they wish regardless of affiliation. Some ACA-affiliated groups on the East Coast are called ACoA.) Even if you do not have alcoholism in your family or do not love a man who abuses alcohol or drugs, ACA programs can teach you how to come to grips with the damage done to you as a child growing up in any kind of dysfunctional home.

In a group setting, members learn how to substitute new beliefs and habits for the harmful beliefs and habits they learned in childhood. Many of the issues discussed in ACA groups—including learning how to set personal boundaries, how to understand feelings of self-hate and move toward self-love, and how to unfreeze feelings—are nearly identical to relationship-addiction issues.

Women Who Love Too Much Groups.   In her landmark bestseller, Robin Norwood gave a step-by-step outline for starting an independent support group. Women in cities across the nation use her book and others as a starting point for sharing and supporting one another's recovery. Some cities have People Who Love Too Much meetings, also based on the Norwood book, attended by both women and men recovering from relationship addiction.

Norwood's book states that developing one's spiritual side is a key step in recovery; thus, some Women Who Love Too Much groups appear to be more spiritually based than others. Depending on how you feel about spiritual issues, you may want to try different groups to see which is right for you.

A nationwide directory of relationship-addiction recovery groups in the United States can be found at the back of this book.

Sex and Love Addicts Anonymous (SLAA) and Sex Addicts Anonymous (SAA).   If addiction to the physical aspect of relationships is a particular problem for you, SLAA and SAA point the way to recovery. Listings for these groups can most likely be found in the white pages of your telephone directory. Alternatively, your state may have a self-help clearinghouse number, which you can obtain by calling the information operator.

Other Support

If you are not interested in or comfortable with the Twelve-Step approach, many women find the help they need from a psychologist familiar with the issue of codependence. If a group setting is not for you, a one-on-one relationship with a therapist can work well.

GETTING THROUGH FIRST DAYS

The first few days of recovery can be unsettling and full of unfamiliar feelings. Perhaps you have just broken up with a lover and are feeling the shock of separation. If you have attended your first recovery group, you may feel stressed to the limit. After their first meeting, some people feel overwhelmed and paralyzed, while others feel relief, as if they've found home.

You may find that because of your loss and the new insights you are experiencing, you simply cannot stop crying. If your first few days are rocky, the following steps can help you to get through them.

- Allow yourself to cry. Don't try to hold back the tears. It is a natural and healing part of the grieving process.

- Give yourself permission to ask for help or affection.

- Tell your friends, "I just need to be heard right now." Friends are often willing to listen. It is all right for you to say, "I just want to tell you how bad I feel right now. You don't have to fix it. Just listen."

- Tell yourself, "I'm going to allow myself to feel bad. I don't have to fix it right now." Let the feelings be. Tell yourself, "This sadness won't destroy me. I won't be stuck here forever. In fact, the more I allow the grieving, the quicker it will heal."

- Let yourself experience exactly what you are experiencing physically and emotionally. If it's sadness you feel, be sad. Avoid telling yourself (or listening to others who say), "You've got to cheer up" or "You've got to snap out of this." Well-meaning people will push good cheer. Others will try to push logic. But putting up a false front will only cut you off from your feelings. Find someone who is simply willing to listen—and understand.

- For now, avoid people who want to "fix" you or who aren't willing or able to hear you. If someone is going through a crisis point in her own recovery, she may not be able to be there for you. Do not take this personally.

DENYING THE PROBLEM

Some women never make it to that first support-group meeting. Instead, they continue to deny that a problem exists. Says Collette Dowling, "It is characteristic of the dependent personality to ignore signs of problems, to examine as little as possible, to endure." Avoidance also occurs when it comes to setting up that first meeting with the therapist.

If you suspect that you are denying that a problem exists or that you are not admitting the severity of the problem, the following exercise can help you learn to see the truth of your situation.

Identifying Denial

The following statements are common forms of denial. Denial is a basic and primitive form of psychological self-defense in which we keep painful facts from our consciousness so that they do not overwhelm us. If you find that you have been using any of these frequently, you are probably unconsciously denying some crucial problem in your experience. Identifying these aspects through the checklist below is the first step toward beginning to see the truth.

Place a check mark next to any statement that triggers a response in you or that sounds like something you have told yourself.

_____ I'm just fine. Everything is fine.

_____ I am the way I am. It's too late for me to change.

_____ If only my (husband, lover, family) would just shape up, then I would be happy.

_____ If I could only find the right person, my life would come together.

_____ If _____ (name) would only stop drinking, then I would be happy.

_____ If I were a better person, I could change my man.

_____ My romantic failures have been all my fault.

_____ My needs are not important.

_____ I am responsible for my family's problems. It's usually my fault when things go wrong.

_____ My role in life is to help others when they are in trouble.

_____ What happened to me in childhood has no effect on my life today.

_____ I shouldn't feel angry. I should always be upbeat.

Identifying Your Truth

Once you have begun to admit what you have denied, you are on the way to recovery.

The following statements may represent your inner truths. They are quite the opposite of the myths we create to keep our denial functioning. As you compare these two lists, ask yourself how your life would be different if you were able to accept your own truth.

_____ I need to make some changes in my life.

_____ It's not too late for me to have a better life.

_____ Only self-change can bring me inner peace. What others do is secondary.

_____ I have to get myself together before I can have a healthy relationship with others.

_____ It would be beneficial if _____ (name) stopped drinking, but my happiness does not depend on the actions of anyone else. I find my own fulfillment.

_____ Only he can change himself. I have power only over my own actions.

_____ I can share responsibility for problems in my past relationships, without putting all the blame on him—or on me.

_____ My needs are as important as anyone else's.

_____ The members of my family are responsible for their own actions and reactions. No one can ruin another person's life.

_____ If I really care about someone, I can be supportive, but I will also give that person the freedom to solve his or her own problems.

_____ What happened to me in childhood affects me today, but with persistence, I can change the beliefs, attitudes, or behaviors I wish to change.

_____ I have a right to all of my feelings, whether they are positive or negative.

MAKING YOUR RECOVERY YOUR FIRST PRIORITY

Robin Norwood advises, "Make your own recovery the first priority in your life."

If you have had low self-esteem, if you have been accustomed to making someone else the focus of your attention, if you have been inclined to make your boyfriend your "god," then you may want to develop new priorities. Right now, your recovery is more important than:

whether or not you meet a new man

whether or not you have a date

whether or not he calls

whether or not you decide to break up with a long-term lover

whether or not your ex-lover comes back into your life

whether or not your friends approve of your support group, your new decisions, or your books on recovery

At one time the comings and goings, the approvals and disapprovals, held importance for you. Now they may seem relatively unimportant, viewed from the perspective of your overall health and well-being.

SIGNS OF RECOVERY

You know you are on your way to recovery when:

- You find the help appropriate to you at your particular stage of the journey. This might be a book on recovery, private or group therapy, or the right support group.

- You form strong, trusting bonds with others traveling along the same path toward recovery. You can share your experiences and learn from others' experiences.

- You learn the difference between caring and caretaking. Even while you encourage others to grow, you know that your primary responsibility is to yourself and your recovery.

- While not blaming yourself for all that goes wrong in a relationship, you are willing to acknowledge your own contributions to problems that have occurred.

- You welcome all your feelings.

- In making decisions about love, you use your mind, your heart, your perceptions, and your intuition.

- You make choices that are best for you, without exploiting anyone else.

- You decide with whom you will spend time and to whom you will become closer. For you, trust grows slowly and appropriately.

- The excitement previously generated by unstable romantic relationships gives way to an interest in growth, serenity, and healthier forms of intimacy.

- Aware of your own painful patterns of the past, you are willing to experiment with new, respectful, and equal relationships with both men and women. If a relationship is not good for you, you are willing to let go of it. You know that any obstacle points out to you what you need to be learning.

- You accept yourself fully. You value your opinions, feelings, appearance, sexuality, and recovery. As your appreciation of yourself increases, you value the uniqueness in others.

PROGRESS, NOT PERFECTION

"True life is lived when tiny changes occur."

TOLSTOY

Recovery from addictive love is not one single event but a very gradual process. During the course of this process you will undoubtedly experience moments that will let you know that your recovery is, indeed, working. Recording these moments can help you to see how far you've come.

Each step toward healthy relationships may feel unnatural to you, as you will be overcoming powerful conditioning. Yet every insight, every look before you leap, every "no" to the negative and "yes" to the positive is a turning point, a decision to choose a better life for yourself. In recovery, no step is small.

Keep a running tab of your own steps forward, writing each one down. The resulting record will help you to appreciate how far you have come and will provide you with concrete evidence of your journey toward recovery.

Donna, a member of my support group, had the following record of positive steps:

I made a New Year's resolution to find a recovery group. I made four phone calls and found one.

I committed myself to go to six meetings. I met Linda and Joyce and we exchanged phone numbers.

I took my niece to the aquarium and the swimaround tank. Then we made valentines for ourselves and our friends.

I decided to take a break—four weeks away from romantic relationships.

I did not get involved with Jerry, a real hunk who said, "I'm not into relationships right now."

I ended the romance with Tim, who criticized my efforts at personal growth.

I told Mark, "I'm mad at you." I told Caroline, "I disagree."

After talking with Jim, I paid attention to how I felt.

My thirty-sixth birthday, sans boyfriend. I celebrated with ten good friends at the dance place. My favorite birthday.

Met Charles at performance theater. We seem to have similar interests. I did *not* tell him my life story in one night. I did tell him, "I like you. I'm a little scared. Let's go slowly."

Now for your record of turning points. Make regular entries, perhaps day by day or week by week.

Identifying Turning Points in My Recovery

_____

_____

_____

_____

_____

_____

_____

_____

_____

_____

_____

_____

_____

_____

_____

_____

_____

_____

_____

_____

_____

_____

_____

_____

_____

_____

_____

_____

The Turning Point: Margo

Thirty-two-year-old Margo has fair skin and rosy cheeks, and she wears her long blonde hair in a topknot. She now lives in Santa Monica and works as an actress and a waitress. Margo has spent most of her life "looking for Daddy—or rescuing somebody." Finally, she is developing a relationship with herself.

I was born in England, the youngest of four. My mother was glamorous and stunning. She was from the lower classes, but she had power in her sexuality. My father was from an upper-class family, but he was weak.

I loved my father terribly and always felt like his special daughter. I was his rescuer. He never abused me but he did abuse my two sisters, and I felt guilty about that.

In later years, I found out that he was an irresponsible alcoholic. My fantasy about my parents was not true.

My mother was the rescuer, my father wanted rescuing. All my life I have played these two roles.

When I was six, my parents' marriage broke up, and I was boarded out to my aunt and uncle. This uncle abused me sexually for five of the eight years I lived with them. When I was thirteen, I ran away from home, looking for my father.

When I was seventeen, I met a man seventeen years older, whom I thought would take care of me. Sex kept us together for two and a half years. He was my drug. I gave my heart, my soul, my mind to this man. In return, I was hospitalized from his abuse. I thought I was to blame.

I had a six-year relationship with a Scandinavian man. There was compassion and humor, but I paid all the bills. When he became unfaithful, I left him and became very promiscuous for about two years. I had this free-floating anger and used alcohol to cover it up.

I met an American man in London, twenty years older, who rescued me financially but not emotionally. I came to the United States.

In all my relationships, I was petrified of letting anyone

know what I needed or wanted. I thought responsibility meant being responsible for others. Even though I was a playgirl, underneath was the idea that I couldn't have a loving relationship, that I didn't deserve one.

Five years ago, I was dying inside. My addiction to alcohol was extreme: I had gone through a few jail incidents and a driving-while-intoxicated charge. I was hitting bottom. I got into Alcoholics Anonymous.

In the first year of that program, I wrote an inventory of all my relationships and saw my life in front of me. Ten months into AA, I got into a love affair and saw how I could be almost instantly obsessed and addicted to a man. That was my turning point. I got on my knees and said, "God, even if you never give me another relationship, I don't want one like this. If I have to live alone, it's fine with me."

I had to come to terms with Margo, and that's what I did for the next two and a half years. I went into therapy and broke down the walls that separated me from the rest of the world, that kept me from being intimate. I confronted my uncle with the incest issue by writing him a long letter. I went to Twelve-Step meetings.

Several years into recovery, I met a man, and for six months we had a honeymoon relationship. But my fear of abandonment kept coming up. Finally, I realized that no one can abandon me—*I* abandon me. It was a wonderful lesson.

Six months ago, when that good relationship turned abusive, emotionally and physically, I got out.

Today, I don't feel addicted to men; I feel attracted to men. I believe you have to come back to *you*. You learn to live with yourself, to exercise, to make friends, to have interests. How on earth would you have time for an addiction?

I was willing to surrender. I had to say, "What I used to do doesn't work. What I want to do is create wholesomeness within myself, so that if I love somebody, it's not going to be from need but from want."

Twelve-Step programs work. With them, I've given up cigarettes, sugar, abusive relationships with men, and drugs. I believe that if you work the Twelve Steps of a recovery program, you can't stay addicted.

Addiction is removed when you're willing to take opposite action. Sitting by the phone waiting for a man to ring, that's not recovery. Actively participating in your own life, that's recovery.

I have nights when I have candlelight and soft music and take a bubble bath. I have one night a week for Margo.

I want a loving relationship. But I'm not willing to have one that includes that kind of pain and addiction.

I had to look at all these painful patterns, to understand where I came from, so I don't have to repeat them. I build up friendships with men so I'm not deprived of male energy. I go to Women Who Love Too Much meetings, to Al-Anon and ACA meetings. I try on a daily basis to put myself first.

Love for me is very different than it was even a year ago. I have fallen in love with the idea of love many times. Now, for me, it's about liking myself so that I can like others—*loving* myself. My relationship with myself is the most important one I have.

CHAPTER 3

Letting Go of Your Obsession with Others

" The more I let go, the more I have. "

Eileen

Relationship addiction means becoming obsessively involved in the life of another person—a lover, a parent, or a friend. In relationship addiction, the other person becomes our drug. We become just as dependent on our lover as an addict is on a substance, and we suffer the pain of withdrawal when we try to give up the addiction.

It is not easy to break the cycle of relationship addiction— yet it can be done. Breaking the cycle of addiction is often called "letting go." Here, this means letting go of overinvolvement in the lives of others. It means letting go of depending on others for approval and of the need to have others act in certain ways.

Letting go also means releasing your control of others. Relationship addicts are secretly afraid that if they stop controlling others, they will lose everything. In reality, quite the opposite often happens, with our relationships *enhanced* by our new attitude.

As of today, consider yourself "fired" from the silent, unspoken second job you have assigned yourself all your life: you no longer must solve your lover's problems, save your family, or

37

be the hero of the world. You no longer need to do what you always felt you *had* to do. You now have choices.

If you have been living for others, now is the time to start living for yourself. This may sound simple, but it can be very difficult. When we have been living our lives in reaction to others' needs, desires and feelings, it can be very hard to start paying attention to our own needs, desires and feelings.

The turning point at this stage of your recovery comes when you can take the focus off everyone else and put the focus on yourself. How will you know when you have put the focus on yourself? This is very easy to tell. Your conversation will no longer be about "him." It will not be about what "they" did to you. Your conversation will stop sounding like "My boyfriend," "My husband," or "My lover says . . . " Your conversation will more likely concern the insights you are discovering about yourself as new phases of your life unfold.

Some people think their relationships will self-destruct if they are not working on them all the time. But a healthy relationship, like a healthy body, does not require such obsessive attention. If you are not involved in a romantic relationship, you can let go of living your life around your parents, your children, or your friends. You can bring the focus back where it belongs—on yourself.

LOVING DETACHMENT

> ❝ I am spiritually connected to my husband and children. I am not emotionally embroiled in their problems. ❞
>
> NINA

The Al-Anon program offers a remarkable tool for letting go, called Loving Detachment. To detach definitely does not mean to end a relationship. It simply means to unhook from compulsiveness in that relationship. Detaching does not mean not caring. What it does mean is not needing desperately and not obsessing.

An attitude of detachment implies that you see clearly the division between "his problems," "my problems," and "our problems"—and that you refuse to take on his problems, such as drug or alcohol addiction. You grant your lover the respect that says he can solve his own problems.

Detachment also means taking care of your own needs. It means knowing that you don't have to take care of anybody else. It means refusing to lie to protect somebody else. It means examining a situation and consciously deciding what your responsibilities are to your husband or lover, children, parents, and friends.

Even if you love someone, you don't have to think for him or feel his feelings for him. You are not responsible for his happiness.

The following exercise can help you to become conscious of the beliefs necessary for practicing loving detachment.

1. Because I love _____ (name), I can give him the freedom

   to _____ as he pleases.

2. Because I love and respect _____ (name), I am going to

   let him solve his own _____.

3. I care about _____ (name), but I am not responsible for

   his financial situation.

4. I do not need to protect _____ from the consequences

   of his _____.

5. Because I love and respect _____ (name), I am going to

   allow him the freedom to make his own _____.

6. I do not have to be in the middle between _____ and

   _____ so that they get along with each other and keep

   the peace.

7. Little by little, I am letting go of overinvolvement in

_____'s life.

As you make these promises to yourself, remember that they do not mean you stop loving. You simply stop obsessing.

THE "FIXER"

> **"** I can be most helpful to others by doing what is best for me. **"**
>
> ERICA

Many women who grew up in alcoholic or dysfunctional families learned to be rescuers, or "fixers." They were compelled by family circumstances to be five-year-old marriage counselors or twelve-year-old special-duty nurses. Often, their parents were unable to perform fully as adults. Thus, the children were forced to give up certain aspects of childhood and to become caretakers prematurely.

This "save-the-day" attitude can become compulsive and self-defeating in adulthood. It can wreak havoc with intimate relationships, in which the tendency is to confuse love with pity and therefore to try to rescue those we love. When we behave in this way, after a while all our energy reserves are depleted and we have little left to give to others—much less to ourselves.

Rescuers often carry this tendency to save others into all of their relationships. Not only do they try to rescue coworkers, but they also try to rescue a lover from his heartless boss, find jobs for their friends, and continually "fix" troubled family members. Because they are so familiar with this behavior, many codependents enter the helping professions (for example, medicine or counseling). Although their motivations may be healthy, they often have an underlying need to fix or rescue others.

This next exercise will help you to let go of the compulsion to fix or rescue. Recovery from the rescue syndrome involves bringing the focus of your life back to you. If you are worried about others' problems, you may well be ignoring your own. Those who "save" others may first need to save themselves.

1. Instead of worrying about _____'s health, I will get to work on my own recreation, diet, and exercise needs.

2. When I'm worried about _____'s financial situation, I will take a closer look at my own budget and financial goals.

3. If I'm worried about _____'s addictions, I will take a look at my own bad habits with food, drugs, or alcohol.

4. If I'm worried about satisfying _____ sexually, maybe I will speak to him about my own needs concerning sex.

5. If I'm worried about _____'s recovery, I can put the focus on my own recovery.

CEREMONIES FOR LETTING GO

> **"**I had to give up the dream of the handsome prince who drives up in his white Mercedes to save me from my cares and woes. **"**
>
> STEPHANIE

Sometimes, in order to let go of obsessions with other people's lives, we must first let go of deeply entrenched ways of thinking, feeling, and behaving. Giving up any behavior pattern or habit, even one you really want to let go of, may feel like losing an old, familiar friend. For this reason, many people like to have a private funeral ceremony in order to acknowledge and express their grief. When Marcia was divorced, she buried the letter in which Joe had asked her to marry him. Sheila buried a bracelet that represented her former commitment to her boyfriend.

Of course, just the thought of breaking up with your lover may bring up the old fear: "I will be alone forever." If so, comfort yourself by remembering the words of Jacquelyn Small:

"The soul needs [the old relationship] to die so room can be made for another relationship that is more appropriate for tasks of the present."

Perhaps you need to release a fantasy that cannot be realized. Sometimes a part of your belief system must die in order for you to have a healthy relationship. Of course, it may be hard to let go of certain fantasies ("I've finally found the perfect man, and I'm so perfect that he'll love me forever"). One of the best ways to come to grips with why you are holding on to this illusion is to find out the part that it plays in your inner life. To start that process, ask yourself these questions (write out both the questions and your answers):

1. What's so appealing about this fantasy?

_____

_____

_____

2. What would be the consequence if I gave up this fantasy?

_____

_____

3. If this fantasy is about perfection, what is so frightening about an imperfect him and an imperfect me?

_____

_____

It is also important that you learn to distinguish between realistic expectations and romantic myths. How much of what you want is fairy-tale fantasy—a young girl's dreams fed by television, movies, and romance novels? How much of it involves healthy, hopeful expectations for a better future relationship?

Weighing the costs and benefits of your dream or habit can help you to see more clearly why you hold on and what would permit you to let go.

The next exercise will help you to differentiate realistic expectations from romantic myths. It can be done either in your group or on your own.

Read through this list and check any sentence that triggers a reaction somewhere inside you.

A lover will:

_____ enhance my life

_____ make me happy

_____ provide companionship

_____ provide affection

_____ provide emotional support

_____ make me feel secure

_____ provide the fun in my life

_____ listen and understand

_____ meet all my needs for affection

_____ provide a sex life

_____ provide sensuality in my life

_____ give me a beautiful home

_____ be strong for me

_____ provide excitement

_____ provide glamour

_____ provide friends

_____ be my close, caring friend

_____ consider me the number-one person in his life, after himself

_____ prevent loneliness

_____ change the way I see myself

_____ be the one who gets angry

_____ be the competent one

_____ provide all of my emotional needs

_____ allow me to connect emotionally, physically, and spiritually with someone I care about

Circle what you feel are the most realistic, healthy expectations in the above list. You may want to hold on to these, since they may guide you in choosing a healthy relationship. List your realistic expectations here.

I expect that my lover will:

1. _____

2. _____

3. _____

4. _____

5. _____

If there are any unrealistic expectations or fantasies you want to let go of, write out each impossible expectation on an index card. These cards will become part of the burial ceremony that follows.

How to Bury the Past

The following exercise can help you put a symbolic end to old feelings and relationships. Here are some ways to mark this occasion with a private ceremony.

Step 1.   If you are breaking up with a lover, you will first want to collect the physical items from the relationship that have emotional charge for you—letters, photographs, items of clothing, and so on. If you are releasing a fantasy, gather the symbolic objects (for example, a calendar or gift).

Write down what you are releasing. When one person in our group performed this ceremony, she wrote:

"I release my attachment to Robert and to my dream of spending my life with him."

Step 2.   Next, prepare your ceremony. Place the items or the written-out statement in a fireplace or a large ashtray.

Step 3.   Then, perform the ceremony. Set the fire and watch the flame burn your papers and other objects. Let yourself feel the feelings—anger, sorrow, resignation, relief.

Los Angeles therapist Rhoda Pregerson suggests an addition to this exercise that helps people to preserve any positive elements from the old relationships. As you review memories of your ex-lover, write each memory on an index card. This may take several days, or even weeks. Next, sort through the cards, separating the ones you are ready to release from those you want to keep. Then perform the fire ritual with those you want to discard. The ones you keep represent the good parts of the relationship, those aspects that you want to carry over into your next involvement.

Alternatively, you might choose to bury your memories in a box in your backyard, as a friend of mine did. Dig a shallow "grave," cover the box with dirt, and add fresh flowers if you want to!

Let the feelings come up. By permitting them to surface, you can better release them.

Step 4.   Now make a simple statement to help you release your fantasy, obsession, or habit. Here are a few examples:

"I lay to rest my fantasy that my lover and I will marry and have a family."

"I lay to rest my fantasy that my old lover will come back into my life."

"I lay to rest my fantasy that meeting the right man can bring me inner peace."

"I lay to rest the idea that if I join a recovery group, then my lover will, too."

"I lay to rest the need to get my mother to approve of me."

"I lay to rest my need to save my father from alcoholism."

"I lay to rest my belief that I am responsible for the success of my daughter's marriage."

POSITIVE HABITS

> " I used to put all of my dreams in one basket. Now I scatter my dreams in many baskets. "
>
> SUSAN

When you are letting go of old beliefs and habits and beginning to replace them with positive ones, this is a sure sign that you are on the road to recovery.

You will know this is happening when (check any breakthrough you have already had):

_____ You can listen to a friend's problem—just listen—and not try to rescue him or her.

_____ Instead of being focused solely on one person, you are interested in many people.

_____ Instead of returning to the "scene of the crime"—where your ex-lover lives, or special places the two of you went to—you find more interesting places to visit.

_____ If you desire something or someone who is not available, you enjoy something or someone who is.

_____ Instead of putting up with abuse, you say no to the relationship.

_____ If you have just broken up with a lover, and he always called at a certain time, you find another pleasurable pursuit to do at that time.

_____ You stop blaming yourself for what others do. You take 100 percent of the responsibility for your own actions and let others do the same for theirs.

_____ Sometimes you may parent your lover, but you also parent yourself.

The Turning Point: Joan

Joan, thirty-two, has large violet eyes and dark-brown hair cut in a short, chic style. She works as a pharmaceutical representative in Boston, where she called on a physician, Jeff, who became her lover.

Joan was involved in a common "loving too much" situation. She shared her lover, Jeff, with another woman. In fact, she knew she was the number-two woman in his life. Yet, she was unable to leave the relationship to form one in which she could be the only woman. When she tried to change the almost exclusively sexual nature of their relationship, her effort met with predictable results. Jeff insisted that he cared and begged her to wait for him a little longer.

Joan was working with a support group at the time and found the courage there to try a terminating ceremony.

The turning point in my recovery happened this week. I got a call from Jeff, who wanted to get together on his sailboat, which had always been an immediate hook. Jeff and I had several romantic routines. One was that I'd go to his house in the morning, and we'd make love before going to work. Then I'd help him change the sheets so that his girlfriend, Marsha, would not know I had been there.

At other times we would go to his boat, drink champagne, and make love. It couldn't have been more romantic. But then I would go back to my lonely house, and he would go back to Marsha.

This week, he called to set up the same plan again. I've been in recovery for six months now, and I did not want to continue to see Jeff in this way. I told him I was unwilling to see him under these conditions. He said, "Can't I get you to come up to the boat?" I said, "No, you can't. But I'll tell you what—if you really want to be with me, let's get together and go to a Red Sox game." He said he was going to get the tickets and would call me Wednesday night. He never called. I was devastated. I called a friend in our support group to talk about it and she suggested that I try a ceremony.

In my bedroom was a stuffed pelican hanging from the ceiling that Jeff had given me because I live on Pelican Lane. I had always had a strong attachment to this gift. I ripped it down from the ceiling, took out a knife, and cut it up. That night, I felt so much pain at what I had been willing to settle for. Perhaps for the first time I was truly paying attention to what it felt like to be a second-class person. Some part of me had not thought I deserved more than a sneaking-around relationship.

When my self-esteem was low, I used to look at photographs of Jeff to fill me up. That night, I gathered the pelican, the photos, and everything in the house that represented Jeff. In my nightgown, at one o'clock in the morning, I threw all of it into the garbage bin and said good-bye. I felt "clean" for the first time in several years.

This morning I worked out at the club, made phone calls, and did things to be of service to people. I don't feel the void today.

Learning to Nurture Yourself

" Now when I get uptight, I ask myself what I need, what I want, and what I feel. I may find that I want to take a walk, get a massage, or be with a friend—and I'll do it. "

SHAKTI GAWAIN

When we love others too much, we often do not nurture ourselves enough. Many of us did not receive enough nurturing as children. We may have been taught to think that our own needs were unimportant. As a result, many of us ignore both our physical and emotional needs, concentrating instead on meeting the needs of others. In the process, we often become exhausted and thus have little energy left for ourselves. This can lead to physical illness, depression, or feelings of resentment when others do not give back to us what we have given them.

It is not selfish to nurture our bodies and our spirits. In fact, only after we have nurtured ourselves can we be genuinely and freely loving toward others. During this stage of recovery, you will learn to take a more active role in nourishing yourself.

In order to learn this, you will need to do two things. The first is to get in touch with your "inner child"; the second is to develop the ability to be a nurturing parent to this inner child.

"All the changes that come to my clients will come from nurturing themselves," says Los Angeles therapist Emile Cacho.

"Sometimes we do need other people to nurture us, but that's just the bridge." Real change comes when you begin to nurture yourself.

YOUR INNER CHILD

Your inner child is comprised of the feelings and thoughts you had as a child. This part always exists inside you, along with all the other parts or visions you hold of yourself (such as your inner parent, which is modeled on the messages your parents gave you, and your inner teacher, modeled on the influential teachers in your life).

As W. Hugh Missildine, M.D., writes in *Your Inner Child of the Past,*

> The child you once were continues to survive inside your adult shell. Whether we like it or not, we are simultaneously the child we once were, who lives in the emotional atmosphere of the past and often interferes in the present, and an adult who tries to forget the past and live wholly in the present. The child you once were can balk or frustrate your adult satisfactions, embarrass and harass you, make you sick—or enrich your life.

Whatever nurturing, attention, validation, or love you feel you did not receive as a child still remains as a hunger within your inner child. Likewise, whatever insecurities, uncertainties, or lack of self-esteem that child experienced still influences your adult personality and affects the way in which you respond to daily events.

Perhaps you are familiar with an inner punishing parent. If your parents were overly critical of you, your inner punishing parent is quick to point out your flaws and remind you of past mistakes ("You failed again—can't you ever learn?" "What's the matter with you?"). It is this inner punishing parent who often deprives us of a sense of self-worth by constantly focusing on our flaws and failing to notice our virtues.

To counter your punishing parent and develop your own sense of self-worth, you will need to learn how to contact the voice of your inner loving parent, that part of you modeled on the nurturing behavior of your parents (or another adult). It is this loving inner parent who praises and encourages you, gives you credit, and is always in your corner ("Well done," "That's very nice," "Congratulations!").

The more you develop your inner loving parent, the greater your feeling of self-worth will be. When this happens, you will no longer need the approval of others in order to feel good about yourself.

The exercises provided for this purpose are very simple and may at first seem a bit childish. But do not be fooled into thinking they're unimportant. They are designed to help you get in touch with your inner child and to speak to that child in the simple language she understands. Stay with these exercises, and you may be surprised at the results.

Contacting Your Inner Child

Once you have learned to contact your loving parent more than your punishing parent, your inner child can begin to feel more secure. When the inner child feels secure, she will not feel a need to look to others for security all the time.

PUNISHING PARENT	LOVING PARENT
You gave everything to him, and the relationship still didn't work out. There must be something wrong with you.	You gave it your best shot; you just didn't know then what you know now.
He didn't return your phone call. That means he doesn't care about you. Maybe he's right—you *are* too needy.	Maybe he's gone away for the weekend. You can call someone else.
You wanted that friend to nurture you, but she seemed angry with you. You must have done something wrong.	Maybe she was rushed or in a bad mood. You can nurture yourself instead.

If we remain dependent on others for a sense of security, we end up having to direct all our actions toward seeking their approval. The security we derive from this is not deep or lasting, since it comes from the outside, not from within. A true sense of security cannot come from anyone else. It is something we give to ourselves.

As someone who grew up in a dysfunctional family, you probably had no deep inner sense of security as a child. Perhaps because of parental alcoholism or frequent fighting, you grew up feeling you were constantly threatened by frightening, chaotic forces that you could not predict or control. Maybe you feared that your parents would abandon you. This is still one of childhood's great fears. Every child needs complete security. You can give yourself this solid sense of security by nurturing the frightened child within you.

The following exercise will help you to contact and reassure your inner child.

If you have a photograph of yourself when you were a child, take it out and look at it. If you don't have one, try to visualize yourself as a child in some familiar setting. Pretend that this little girl is alive inside you. If you have difficulty imagining yourself as a child, go to a playground and watch, or listen to a child on the bus. This may trigger those childlike feelings.

In talking to your inner child, start out slowly. If you haven't spoken with her in thirty years, there may be some awkward moments. If you have ignored her, apologize and ask her forgiveness. Your honesty will help seal your friendship.

Ask your inner child about the things that make her feel insecure or afraid. Really explore the answers until you feel that you have arrived at some basic truth about the things that upset you as a child.

Then, let your loving parent reassure your inner child. You might say, "Don't worry; it will be all right. I love you. I won't hurt you. You're safe with me."

Ask your inner child if she is afraid of being abandoned. You will probably find that she is. This can be an overwhelming emotional experience for you; a child who lives in fear of losing a parent experiences acute terror. Reassure her that you will never leave her, and that you will always be there for her.

Ask the child what her dreams are. Ask her, too, what she wants to do right now, and listen to her. Perhaps she needs some time off from responsibilities. Perhaps she wants to run in the park or swim in the ocean. Give her some, though not all, of what she asks for, as you would with any child.

Let yourself become aware of your inner child at quiet moments of the day. When you are driving, imagine that she's sitting next to you in the car. Play the kind of music she likes to hear. Sing with her. Let her know that you love her and enjoy her company.

When she is lively, join in the fun. When she is upset, speak gently to her. Simply be interested in her—in what she has to say and how she feels.

When you find yourself feeling frightened or insecure, ask your inner child how she's feeling. Chances are, you'll find that it is *she* who is feeling insecure. When this happens, let your loving parent reassure her.

LETTERS TO YOURSELF

Childhood is not the only time in our lives when we feel vulnerable. As a teenager, you may have felt overwhelmed by a parent's alcoholism or other severe problem. You need to be able to talk to—and comfort—this self.

Write a letter to your inner self at a critical point (adolescence, early twenties, or a period of intense crisis or transition in your life). Ask yourself what you would have benefited from hearing at that time. Then express that in the letter. In this way, you can reparent yourself from the vantage point of your current wisdom.

For example, you might tell your teenage self that:

She is okay exactly as she is.

She is attractive.

She is likable.

She is talented.

She is as valuable as her brother or sister.

She deserves boyfriends who treat her well.

LOVING YOURSELF ENOUGH

One way in which you can parent your inner child is by setting in motion a daily habit of loving action toward yourself. Once you have practiced this for a while, it will become automatic, reinforcing your self-respect and self-approval. Answer the following questions with "always," "often," "rarely," or "never": Do I love myself enough:

to speak only kind words to myself? _____

to let go of harmful relationships? _____

to seek friendship and support from others who are on the path of growth? _____

to have empathy for myself and my situation? _____

to consider my needs to be as important as anyone else's?

_____

to set limits and say, "Yes, that behavior is okay, but do not cross this line"? _____

to hold out for a relationship with someone who can be a real partner to me? _____

For every entry you marked "rarely" or "never," be aware that these are areas you may want to work on.

Learning to Love Your Body

Just as your inner child needs to be nurtured, so does your "outer child"—your body. Perhaps you have been taught to ignore the messages your body sends. But if you slow down and listen, you will find that your body is always telling you what it needs. Pay attention to how your body feels, and give it what it needs to feel nurtured, pampered, and loved.

In the following exercise, place a check mark next to any suggestion that triggers a physical reaction. Ask your body if it would like to:

_____ go to a quiet place or relax in a comfortable chair

_____ take a bath, or have a pedicure or facial

_____ be rubbed with lotion or oils

_____ enjoy sexual pleasure, either with your partner or alone

_____ have a massage

_____ wear clothes in colors that feel right for today and fabrics that feel good on your skin

_____ get some fresh air, perhaps by taking a walk by the ocean or in the woods

Practice this exercise by doing at least one of these activities (or some other activity you find pleasurable) each day.

Asking for Help

One important way to nurture yourself is by learning to ask for help when you need it. As a woman who loves too much, you are probably so accustomed to keeping your own needs bottled up that asking someone for help may seem frightening, even overwhelming. To feel more at ease about this, remember that you are not asking to be saved, and that the other person has the freedom to say no. You may be turned down, but often there is healing even in asking.

Say each of these sentences out loud, imagining the intended listener:

1. (To a stranger) "Will you help me lift the hood of my car?"

2. (To a friend) "I'm moving this weekend. Would you be able to help me take one carload to my new place?"

3. (To your sister) "I'm swamped. Can you help me plan this party for Jenny?"

4. (To your partner) "Honey, are you willing to pick up after yourself?"

Which, if any, was difficult for you to say?

_____

_____

_____

What feelings came up when you said this? (examples: guilt, fear, resentment)

_____

_____

_____

What feeling memory from your past makes it difficult for you to ask for help? (For example, perhaps your first husband acted helpless and expected you to do everything.)

_____

_____

_____

What are the advantages of your asking for help? (for instance, increasing self-esteem, respecting your own needs)

_____

_____

_____

What are the disadvantages of asking for help? (possibly inconveniencing someone, risking rejection, making waves)

_____

_____

_____

Expressing Preferences

If saying what you need seems too intimidating at the moment, perhaps you can start by learning to express preferences.

A preference is not a lecture or a sermon. It is a one- or two-sentence statement conveying your want or need. You can get more of your needs met—without manipulating or controlling—by simply stating your preferences. Remember that you are no longer trying to change someone's fundamental nature with your request. You are, instead, focusing on yourself. In fact, the other person has the right to refuse you. But if your request is reasonable, a reasonable person will likely consider your need.

This exercise will help you know how comfortable you are in stating preferences.

Say each of these sentences out loud, imagining the intended listener:

1. (To a counter clerk) "I'd like that croissant right there, some butter and jam, and extra napkins, please."

2. (To a friend) "Let's stop for a cold drink. I'm really thirsty."

3. (To your mother) "I'd prefer it if you did not give me advice."

4. (To your lover) "I don't like sarcasm. I'd prefer it if you would say things directly."

Which, if any, was difficult for you to say?

_____

_____

_____

What feelings came up? (examples: guilt, fear, resentment)

What feeling memory from your past makes it difficult for you to state preferences? (For example, perhaps your opinions were often devalued by a family member.)

What are the advantages of stating your preferences? (increasing self-esteem, respecting your needs, and so on)

What are the disadvantages of stating your preferences? (possibly inconveniencing someone, risking rejection, making waves)

PROGRESS IN NURTURING

You will know that you are beginning to love yourself when (check any breakthroughs you have experienced):

_____   You spend a day alone—and notice how that feels.

_____   You feel down or defeated, and you ask yourself: What would a loving mother do for a child who feels the way I do?—and then you do it for yourself.

_____   You are loyal to yourself. In a disagreement, you can see another person's point of view but are still able to see your own.

_____   You think of something you would like to get for yourself—a piece of jewelry, some fancy lingerie, or another special gift— and you make a special effort to get it.

_____   You feel ill, and you immediately begin to pamper yourself.

_____   You think twice about doing something that, while it would likely have some positive effects, could also cause you harm.

_____   When you laugh, it is a genuine laugh.

_____   You achieve a success of some kind, but you don't reject or make light of it. In fact, you let other people know of your success.

_____   Someone rejects you, but you don't take it personally. Instead, you realize that the problem might well be the other person's.

_____   You have the courage to ask for what you want in the way of sex or affection.

The Turning Point: Faith

Faith, forty-three, is a petite, exotic-looking Oriental woman with golden-apricot skin, almond-shaped eyes, and glossy black hair. She has worked as a secretary at a submarine base and as a welder. She is now an Atlanta housewife with three children.

Like many women who love too much, Faith is an incest

survivor. She was abused not only by her father, but also by her brother and sister. As is typical of women from dysfunctional families, Faith had very low self-esteem and did not believe that she deserved to experience the pleasures of sex and love.

Predictably, the first two husbands she chose were exciting but abusive. Her third marriage was to Greg, a navy captain. Greg was a good but very serious and highly disciplined man who criticized Faith frequently. The couple had separated.

By bonding with women in her support group and learning from them, Faith was able to grow. This was a consequence of her own self-acceptance, for it was only after she began to thoroughly accept and value herself—her appearance, her sexuality, her wants and needs—that she was able to truly love another person.

When I first joined the group, my marriage was rocky, and Greg and I had separated. We were blaming each other for our problems, and I was sexually unsatisfied. My self-esteem was low. I had a very difficult time accepting Greg as he was and constantly tried to change him. It took me a long time to realize that this was because I had not accepted myself.

My first step toward self-acceptance was joining the women's group. Because of the incest issue with my sister, I had never trusted women. But the people in our group, traveling on the same path, learn to love and encourage one another. I was able to form strong bonds with these women, and I grew to feel that they accepted me.

Once I felt safe with them, I began to feel more safe with my own femininity. My inner child, that innocent young girl who had been so abused, slowly began to come alive again. I wanted to play more often, even to be silly. I began to feel more creative and free to be myself.

The next step was accepting my own sexuality. I had always thought that I was not attractive enough to enjoy sexual pleasure. I thought the pleasures of sexual love belonged only to tall, pretty, young, thin, blonde women. But in our group I met women who had that kind of beauty who also did not feel worthy of sexual pleasure. Many of these women were also incest survivors. What was encouraging was that these women had worked through this problem. Now they were unashamed of their sexuality. This gave me hope.

Sexually, I had always been a performer and a pleasure-giver. I had read all the books on how to give pleasure to a man, but I had never asked for anything for myself. I was an observer on the sidelines, not getting involved in sexual feelings, even burying my sexual feelings with food. Though I had been married to two men for a total of more than twenty years, I had never achieved an orgasm.

Greg and I started seeing each other again. I had always thought he should be psychic about my needs. I thought, "If he loved me, he'd know what I want." But after listening to women in our group speak about communicating with their lovers, I began to tell him specifically what I wanted from him, sexually and in other ways. I would say, "When you do such and such, I feel such and such." I had to acknowledge that I had sexual feelings, and that this was okay. At forty-one, I started to be sexually satisfied.

Sexual satisfaction was important to my self-acceptance, but the turning point came after Greg had moved back into our house. I told him that in the mornings I needed him to just hold me—not to be sexual, but to be comforting. People who were abused or neglected as children have an almost insatiable need to be held. He understood. We would set the alarm early and hold each other for a half hour. At last, I began to feel loved and cherished.

For the first time, I started noticing my own beauty. When I had stopped working, I had also stopped taking care of my looks. But now I started walking every day and fixing my hair in new ways. I began to notice little things in the mirror, such as that my skin had a nice texture. I listened to myself in the group and knew that I was articulate. My friends often told me that I was warm and lively and kind. I saw a new photograph of myself, and I could see that I was attractive. As I began to value myself, I made up an affirmation that I said every day: "I, Faith, am a beautiful woman, inside and out, worthy of recovery."

When I could accept myself as I was for that day, I could

accept Greg as he was for that day. Before, I had always focused on his flaws. But fixing his shortcomings is not my job. I'm so busy working on my own recovery that I hardly have time to notice his shortcomings. Sometimes he moves so slowly that I could strangle him, but I see that it's really my own impatience I need to work on.

Once I had accepted him completely, Greg started to relax. He stopped being so critical. Now he laughs and jokes and hugs people. He knew he was not as witty as my ex-husband, so he would cut out cartoons of "Cathy" and "The Far Side" to make me laugh. I appreciated that. I began to feel warmer toward him.

All my life, I had been chasing the silver bauble of the perfect relationship. I got the idea from books and movies. It was a mirage. One day I woke up and realized that I loved Greg, that I had a good marriage, and that I had the relationship I wanted.

CHAPTER 5

Releasing the Patterns of the Past

> " When an inner situation is not made conscious, it appears outside as fate. "
>
> C. G. JUNG

Many codependents feel trapped by the past. They fear they are destined to repeat the negative, self-defeating patterns they learned during childhood. But this need not be so. We *can* change the present, by releasing the past and breaking through to new, healthier patterns.

It's important to remember that in excursions to the past, we are not seeking to blame our parents or other family members. We are simply trying to see clearly what happened and how it affects us today. If we are blaming anything, it is the disease of alcoholism or the process of dysfunction.

We cannot expect to fully resolve in this chapter all that has gone on in the past. However, the exercises offered here can help to further your progress in an ACA group or with a private therapist or therapy group. If you are not currently in a support group or seeing a therapist, wait until such a support system is in place before doing these exercises.

If you grew up in a dysfunctional family, it is likely that you suffered principal psychological damage in one or both of the following ways: (1) you were assigned a rigid, narrowly defined role, one that you are still fulfilling today; or (2) you were constantly cut off from your real emotions by the message, "Don't feel." The legacy of such damage sabotages healthy adult relationships.

Still, you may be asking: Why examine the wounds of the past? Why dredge up so many moments that are painful to remember? The answer is that by consciously identifying your unhealthy patterns and the conditions that created them, you can shed new light on what once lay below your conscious awareness. By systematically defusing the past in this way, you can live more freely in the present.

Once you can see how dysfunction in the family system set up these negative patterns, you can begin to release the painful emotions that accompany these patterns—for example, by expressing your anger and hurt and by sharing your story with others. As the process of recovery unfolds, you will begin to see your past without filters. You will see and accept what happened. You will make peace with your past. And you will start to live more fully today.

FAMILY ROLES

> "I was a Cinderella who never went to the ball."
>
> KAREN

When we are limited in our emotions, we may also be limited to a confining role that prevents us from healthy intimacy in adulthood. No role is healthy, no matter how glamorous or heroic it may appear.

Many codependents are surprised to learn that they are still playing out the same limited roles they played in childhood. The scapegoat still takes the blame for everything that goes wrong in a relationship. The parent or little mother, who in childhood had to shoulder responsibilities for others but was not taken care of by others herself, still plays the caretaker in her relationships. The placater, who tried desperately to make peace in her troubled family, tries only to appease her lovers and doesn't communicate with them about whatever negative feelings she may have.

Perhaps the most poignant role of all is that of the victim. The woman who was physically or sexually abused often grows up to form abusive relationships. In her family, she learned that abuse was the only expression of love and attention she could receive; as an adult, therefore, she seeks out men who show love in this familiar yet distorted way. Others think that a lack of physical abuse in a relationship automatically means that the relationship is healthy. As a result, such women allow themselves to be emotionally abused.

This set of exercises will help you to identify your role or roles so that you can break out of the limitations they place on your adult relationships.

1. Put a check mark next to the words that best describe the role or roles you remember playing in your family.

_____ Rescuer (is always attempting to save others from disasters of their own or another's making)

_____ Scapegoat (takes responsibility for all that goes wrong)

_____ Mascot (distracts, makes everyone laugh)

_____ Victim (victim of physical, emotional, or sexual abuse)

_____ Rebel (defies authority)

_____ Heroine (always demonstrates courage and high principles)

_____ Beauty Queen (admired for looks alone)

_____ The Brain (high academic achiever)

_____ Little Mother (nurtures others)

_____ Helper (attempts to control others by helping them)

_____ Placater (soothes ruffled feelings; acts as family therapist)

_____ Lost Child (not noticed or seen; ignored)

2. Now that you have identified your role or roles, try to remember the circumstances that created them, and answer the following questions:

When you were a child, who took care of you?

_____

_____

Whom did you take care of?

_____

_____

At what age did you become a caretaker?

_____

_____

What form was this care permitted to take? (for example: making the other person laugh, soothing his or her feelings, downplaying your own achievements, distracting, rescuing a victim, taking all the blame or responsibility)

_____

_____

_____

3. Today, what are the advantages of the role you now have? (familiarity, pleasing my family, avoiding responsibility, getting attention, acting helpless, being taken care of)

_____

_____

_____

4. What are the disadvantages of the role you now have? (confining, limiting, makes me unhappy, keeps me a victim, makes me devalue my worth, too much responsibility, unfair expectations)

_____

_____

_____

5. What do you want to change about your role? (expand it, eliminate it, restrict it to certain situations)

_____

_____

_____

6. What have you done to reinforce this role? (surrounded myself with people who see me in this one role; engaged in negative self-talk—for instance, "Oh, I'm just the family loser")

_____

_____

_____

7. What steps have you already taken to expand your role? (going to ACA meetings, seeing a therapist, reading, surrounding myself with friends who see "all of me")

_____

_____

_____

8. Apart from your family role, who are you really?

_____

_____

_____

9. What more innovative roles would you like to adopt? (Check one or more of the following.)

_____   collaborator

_____   learner

_____   teacher

_____   playmate

_____   partner

_____   artist

_____   coach

Once you have expanded your roles, you can eliminate roles altogether—and simply be yourself.

IDENTIFYING YOUR FORBIDDEN FEELINGS

> **"** Get it up, get it out, get it over. **"**
>
> A TWELVE-STEP SLOGAN

Healthy relationships span the whole spectrum of human emotions. Unhealthy relationships are closed off, frozen into a pattern of "acceptable" feelings. When you learn to experience and express all your feelings, no matter how uncomfortable you are with them, you will be able to be more accepting of what your partner is feeling. As a result, your relationship will be much healthier.

Most codependents grew up in families in which they were denied expression of at least one or more major feelings—anger, love, dislike, compassion, and so on. These restrictions were reinforced by the roles they were given to play. For example, if you were the family hero, perhaps you could never ask for nurturing; if you were the scapegoat, perhaps you were never allowed to feel proud of your accomplishments; if you were the mascot, perhaps you were never allowed to show sadness.

The following exercise will help you to say what you could not say, and to feel what you could not feel.

Close your eyes and think of the house you lived in as a child. Picture the outside of the house, as if you were standing in the front yard. Now, in your mind's eye, go inside the house. Picture yourself in the living room or kitchen. Someone in your family says something unpleasant to you. You want to speak up, but something stops you. Ask your inner child what is stopping you. Is it an expression on the other person's face? Is it a remark that this person has made? Now return to the present. Try to pinpoint the feeling you wanted to express but could not. Was it anger, fear, hurt, vulnerability, sadness?

To release your forbidden feeling, you may want to write a letter to the person who gave you the message that this particular feeling was not allowed. Here is a letter one group member wrote to her father concerning a forbidden feeling in her childhood:

Dear Dad,

Do you know what it is like to grow up in a house in which I could never be angry? Oh, *you* got to be angry. You could blow up like a volcano, and I had to tiptoe around you for fear of setting you off. But I could never get mad. I was so afraid of your retaliations, of the way you put me down and withdrew.

You wanted me to be sweet and smiling—always. Well, nobody is like that. Not children, not adults, nobody.

Do you know, in later life, how many problems this habit of fake sweetness caused me? It has put up a barrier between me and the rest of the world. Until recently, it was impossible for me to honestly admit to my feelings. And if I can never be real with anyone, then I can never be close to them.

I am human. Sometimes I am sad, and sometimes I am angry. I have a right to each of these feelings.

Although I love you, I have been angry all my life over this—and the only way I can let go of this anger is to express it to you. Please understand my need to get this off my chest. Thank you for listening.

Love,
Melanie

It is unlikely that you will actually want to mail this letter. But if you feel you need closure, you can also write a letter to yourself from that person, imagining what you would most like him or her to say. Here is the "response" Melanie wrote, which was healing for her.

Dear Melanie,

Boy, you really let me have it! You know, I never thought that someone who looked as sweet as you could be seething inside. When I was growing up, girls were not supposed to have ugly feelings. But, of course, you have those feelings, and you have a right to them.

Guess I blew it, and I'm sorry. I do love you. I do care. I'm glad you told me all this. It's hard for me to take right now, but I have the feeling it will bring us closer.

Love,
Dad

RELEASING YOUR FEELINGS

❝ With my husband, I was never allowed to be soft. I always had to be strong. ❞

JOHANNA

During the course of recovery, the very feelings you have been repressing since childhood in order to maintain your assigned role may suddenly come flooding back. This can be a very frightening experience. You may be flooded with a sadness so overwhelming that you feel utterly despairing for a time. Or you may experience an almost uncontrollable anger so violent that you find yourself physically shaking.

As disturbing as these experiences may be, they represent an important new stage in your recovery. They are a sign that you are finally breaking through the artificial barriers created in your childhood, barriers that have always separated you from some of your most important emotions. These feelings need to rise to the surface to be released.

The next exercise will help you to release many more of the so-called "negative emotions."

The following exercise represents methods used by the women in one group for safely releasing these emotions.

First, it is important to avoid "swallowing" or denying your anger—something you may have been doing all your life. If you repress feelings in this manner, they will turn inward and fester, causing you physical or psychological harm. Instead, begin to explore healthy ways of releasing these feelings. When a long-buried emotion threatens to overwhelm you as it surfaces, try taking one of the following steps:

- Do some physical exercise that will redirect the energy, such as playing tennis, jogging, walking, or dancing to lively music.

- Go to an Al-Anon, ACA, or women's group meeting to talk about how you feel.

- Call another woman in your support group and talk about your feelings.

- If no one is available to talk to, visualize an understanding friend and tell that friend everything you are feeling. Imagine this person's response.

- If you feel like crying, give yourself permission to cry. If you feel like screaming, find an appropriate place where you won't disturb others and let go.

- If after trying all of the above, you still need to confront someone directly in order to fully release your feelings, then do so, using "I-talk" ("I'm angry with you!"), rather than "you-talk" ("You're an inconsiderate jerk!"). This will indicate that you're taking responsibility for how you feel and are not blaming the other person.

TAKING TIME TO MOURN

> " This ability to mourn, that is, to give up the illusion of [her] happy childhood, can restore the depressive's vitality and creativity. "
>
> ALICE MILLER

As you release the past, you may feel a sense of loss or disillusionment. These feelings are perhaps based on the following realizations:

- I may have become a caretaker so early that I lost out on being a child. Now I need to grieve for the loss of my childhood.

- My parents may never change. There is no magic key I can come up with that will force them to change to my liking. Not even my recovery will change them.

- I cannot force my parents to go into therapy or into a Twelve-Step program, even if it would really benefit them to do so. That is their choice.

- Even though my mother may have loved me, she may have rejected my real self and instead admired the false, "perfect," well-behaved self she wanted me to be. This may have led to my first early loss of self.

Each of these truths about the past deserves mourning. When the time comes to mourn, set aside time for it. You will likely discover some other truths that are uniquely yours. As Linda Leonard, author of *The Wounded Woman,* writes, "First comes all the pain and rage against the wound. Then, with acceptance of the wound come the tears of transformation and a natural healing that can lead to love and compassion." Write down all your disillusionments and let yourself feel the feelings.

One important aspect of freeing yourself from an unwanted role is recognizing that your parents may never change and, therefore, may never accept your changes. If they are fixed in their ways, they will attempt to play out the same roles and will expect you to carry out your old roles, too. To be free of an unwanted role, you may need to detach yourself formally from

their expectations of you and from your expectations of them.
Here's one technique:

Dear _____:

I, _____, hereby release myself from

the following role in my family (caretaker, beauty queen, res-

cuer, the brain, etc.):

_____

_____

_____
Your signature

Do not sign your declaration of independence until you
feel you can release your parents from responsibility for how
you are today. If you cannot do this, perhaps you need more
time—to release more emotions, or to mourn. If you are not yet
ready for this step, be gentle with yourself, and continue to go
to your group.

MAKING A DECLARATION OF INDEPENDENCE

❝ Finally, I am living my own life. ❞

ENID

Letting go of parental expectations can involve acknowledging
that you will never be able to fill the role your parents wanted
you to play, never become what they wanted you to become.
However, you should not see this as a failure to live up to their
needs, but rather as the first step in reclaiming your self.

In letting go of the expectations my parents and family had
for me,

I do not have to:

_____

_____

I will, however:

_____

_____

_____

You will know that you are releasing the past when you (check any that apply):

_____   Have an equal relationship with your parents.

_____   Create a family of supportive friends.

_____   Feel compassion for your parents, the environment they grew up in, and the messages they were given.

_____   Can tell the difference between anger and hurt, or rejection and abandonment.

_____   Can relate an emotional charge experienced today to a memory from childhood.

_____   Allow yourself to feel the so-called "negative" feelings, and realize the health in this.

_____   Know that, while you may feel all your feelings, you do not need to act them out in ways that will harm you or others.

_____   Do not wait for anyone to release you from old roles or expectations. You release yourself.

_____   Know how to release feelings in ways that are not harmful to you or others.

_____   Do not get "stuck" in one feeling. You can move past it and then go on to the next feeling, and to the next.

_____ Except for excursions into the past for the purpose of releasing it, you are living in the here and now.

The Turning Point: Karin

Karin's father is a prominent trial lawyer who is a social alcoholic—that is, he manages to maintain a "normal" surface life, holding down a job and following a regular routine. A former Olympic wrestler, he is a large man with a loud voice and the presence of a politician. Karin's mother, small and darkly pretty, had been plowed under by her husband's domineering ways. Her means of escape was gambling. She would borrow money from one of her wealthy friends, then call her bookie to bet on horses.

From a very early age, Karin escaped into a world of fantasy. She drew and painted and grew up to be the family artist. In an alcoholic family, the second-oldest child often becomes the family scapegoat, and Karin was also given this role. Today, her parents live in New Jersey and Karin lives in Minnesota, where she is an interior designer.

Karin is tall and pretty, with striking dark eyes. She has attracted literally dozens of boyfriends, but, at thirty-four, has had only one serious relationship. She always sensed that her feelings of resentment toward her father had worked against her having healthy relationships. She was usually attracted to macho men like her father, men whom she would soon grow to despise.

While she was in a recovery program, she and her father met for dinner, and their relationship started to change.

I had always had a bad relationship with my father. Sometimes we didn't speak for years. He seemed to think that bringing me up meant putting me down. When he came to Minneapolis on business, I dreaded seeing him. After an evening with him, I always felt like I'd been put through the wringer.

That night, I met him in a restaurant, and I noticed that the maître d' made a big fuss over him. My father smiled and blushed, and somehow I sensed that this was why he had chosen this particular restaurant. Right then, I started to think: this man needs a lot of attention. I sense a paper tiger behind the macho exterior.

We sat down, and he talked about himself for a good hour. I asked him about his job. Come to think of it, I had never asked him about his work before, because I didn't think it was very interesting. So I was surprised when it was.

As usual, he started barking commands at the waiter, and he sent a lot of dishes back to the kitchen. Before therapy and my group, this would have made me feel crazy. But this time, somehow, it just amused me. I remembered that my father's dad was an alcoholic, too. Being an ACA, my dad was a big controller, and I was seeing this in action. At sixty-seven, he was still as vigorous as he'd been in his wrestling days. I had to admire his spunk.

Then he got into a tirade about my sister, four years older than me, who had quit her job. It turned out that my dad's friend had gotten my sister her job, and my dad thought this looked bad for *him.* Again, I could tell how fragile Dad's ego was, and this surprised me.

I said, "Dad, I can see how it must have looked bad for you for Mary to quit. At the same time, Mary did stay at that job for twelve years." I could see another ACA issue of his: fierce, misdirected loyalty. I did not take his anger personally. I could see that it was his problem.

As the evening moved on, I listened a lot and talked very little. Finally, he confided to me that he had never gotten along with women until he met my mother. And I confided that I had never gotten along with men. We laughed over this double confession. Then he changed the subject and spoke about an upcoming family wedding I did not want to attend. I could feel my body clenching and could sense a battle: he would order me to go. He asked, "Are you going to the wedding?" I answered calmly, "I have other plans that day." That was it. No warfare, and no apology.

Before that night, I had thought my dad was just a blowhard. Now his point of view fascinated me. I thought, "Oh, that's how he sees things." It was a good evening. I wrote him a letter and told him I had never felt closer to him. I'm not sure how he took my letter, for he has always hated "sensitive" men and did not want to appear that way.

Somehow, that night I was detached and yet felt more compassionate. Every woman I know who's in a good relationship has somehow come to terms with her father. I am sure that this softening toward my father will help my relationship with other men, because I'm accepting my father for who he is.

Recovering Wholeness

> " Be really whole
> And all things will come to you. "
>
> LAO TSU

> " When you see all that you have within your-
> self, how can you be lonely? "
>
> SHARON

Many of us who have been overinvolved in the lives of others do not feel complete within ourselves. We mistakenly believe that we need someone else to make us whole. As children, in order to keep the peace in our families or among our friends and schoolmates, we may have given away essential aspects of our personalities or characters—for example, aggressiveness or creativity. As adults, too, we may have given away essential parts of ourselves in order to stay in a romantic relationship. The loss of these vital aspects of our personalities may have led to our present feelings of being incomplete. Some of us may not even believe that these traits were ever a part of our emotional makeup. However, in reality each of us has within us the full range of human capacities, even though some of these aspects may have been, until now, unexpressed.

An important phase of our inner journey involves recovery

of our wholeness. Many women have actually felt a physical difference while doing the exercises that follow, as they begin to feel more complete within themselves.

TIME AWAY FROM RELATIONSHIPS

Recovery from addictive love allows us to begin to know ourselves as whole for the first time. This knowledge is of vital importance: in feeling only partially whole, we have been attracted to people who also felt incomplete. The unhealthy relationships we formed were based on the illusion of mutual completion, with both partners believing that wholeness could be achieved only through a relationship with another.

As you begin to feel less dependent on others to make you whole, you will not need a relationship to help compensate for what you think you lack as a person. Instead, your relationship will enhance the development of the person you already are. In this case, two halves do not make a whole; rather, with two wholes there will be a healthy *two*.

The first step toward recovering wholeness is to take some time away from romantic relationships. Most experts agree that a person cannot recover from addictive patterns in relationships without first taking some time off from romantic interactions.

This time off need not be lengthy, and you need not end your romantic relationship to have it. If you are involved in a relationship, you may simply want to tell your lover that you need time to yourself for a period of your choosing. Some women not currently in relationships decide to spend three or six months on their own. But if you are in a long-term relationship, even a weekend spent on your own can give you a whole new perspective.

This time away from intimate relationships is an important halfway station in your progress. Rarely does a woman who has just left a dysfunctional relationship immediately form a healthy one. Typically, she needs that crucial middle step of separation to allow her to reconnect with herself before it is possible for her to have a truly healthy, mutually independent relationship.

For those who have not spent much time alone, unstructured time without plans or others to care for can prove dismaying, even frightening. Many of us fear loneliness. We fear facing the emptiness we mistakenly think we will find inside. Running away from this loneliness is often what drove us into abusive or unfulfilling relationships in the first place. But as we make contact with the lost areas of our personalities, we discover that we are beginning to enjoy our own company for the first time. More importantly, we come to know and love our whole self. As a result, we are able to love others more fully.

Once we have completed the process of bonding with the disowned parts of ourselves, we become aware that while other people can enhance our lives, we do not need them in order to feel complete. Instead, they enrich our newfound sense of self. We find, too, that we are giving and receiving in healthier ways.

FINDING THE MISSING PIECES

> **"** When we decide to let go of the addiction . . . we draw from within ourselves that quality of the true self that the addiction was masking. **"**
>
> JACQUELYN SMALL

Psychologists say that we tend to pursue in others those parts of ourselves that we have split off or given away. As you examine your romantic "hooks" in the next exercise, you may find clues to aspects of yourself that are missing and that, once reclaimed, can make you whole.

Put a check mark next to those qualities that attract you most strongly in a possible romantic partner (check any items that apply).

_____   Wealth and power

_____   Decisiveness

_____   Playfulness

_____   Emotional self-control

_____   Attractiveness/sex appeal

_____   Creativity/intuition

_____ Worldliness

_____ Spiritual qualities

._____ Intelligence

_____ Organized life

_____ Social adeptness

_____ Athletic dexterity

_____ Aggressiveness

If your "hooks" are wealth and power, perhaps in the past you learned to deny your own inner needs for security. You might seek advice on how to improve your financial picture, or you might want to initiate a small business venture.

If you are magnetized by men who seem to have all the answers, perhaps you learned to distrust your own knowledge and opinions as a child.

If you are hooked by boyish, playful men who refuse to grow up, perhaps the child in you was not given enough free time to play. Your inner child may be craving time to enjoy the diversions you are constantly denying yourself.

If you are drawn to men who possess emotional control, perhaps you were not encouraged to be coolly rational and clear-thinking when the situation demanded it.

If your men must be very handsome, perhaps you need to appreciate your own beauty.

If you are attracted to highly creative men, you may want to pursue your own creative talents and abilities.

RECLAIMING YOUR MISSING PIECES

❝Recovery is getting to know ourselves as whole persons. **❞**

ALISON

In the next exercise, you will go more deeply into how to reconnect and integrate the missing aspects of yourself. This exercise was adapted from pioneering work in psychosynthesis by Italian psychologist Roberto Assagioli and his collaborator and student, Piero Ferrucci.

Close your eyes and imagine a blank screen. On this screen, create an image of your current prominent personality traits (sometimes called subpersonalities). You will be working with only one trait at a time.

Envision each trait as personalized in a man or a woman. In each case, what does he or she look like?

_____

_____

_____

One woman pictured her traits of elegance and business acumen as combined in "The Entrepreneur," a powerful, successful businesswoman clad in a silk suit, wearing pearl stud earrings and expensive perfume. Another saw the heroic side of her, "The Heroine," as a blonde Scandinavian, standing tall and stalwart. Yet another called up her caretaker, "The Nurse," who wore white shoes and was scrubbed and primed for action.

If you have trouble visualizing this kind of image, you may be able to *hear* the dominant personality trait more easily than you *see* it. One woman was able to identify "The Whiner," and another called her character "Perfection."

What voice inside you comes up most often? What does it sound like? Give a name to this subpersonality.

_____

_____

Sometimes a particularly persistent subpersonality is bequeathed to you by one of your parents. Which parent's voice do you hear most often inside of you? Can you give a name to this voice?

Focus on one personality trait you have identified. Picture the character embodying it, and talk to her. Ask her what she wants to tell you. She is always trying to do something good for you, even though she may at first appear negative or destructive. Ask her what she is trying to do for you, and write her answer here.

One woman asked her subpersonality "Scaredy Cat" the question, "Why are you always so scared?" The subpersonality told her, "Because Mom was away so much, and I never had much mothering as a child." Through this, the woman was able to see that she needed nurturing and comforting. This part of her was trying to compel her to seek what she needed.

Another talked to "Fussy Mabel" and found out that this aspect of her personality was trying to save her from rejection. Fussy Mabel believed that neatness was the ticket to acceptance. Now that she understood Fussy Mabel, she did not feel she had to placate her.

Another woman in recovery called her dominant voice "King Ed." By talking with him, she found out that this subpersonality believed he would lose all his power if he were not *always* right. But now that she understood this personality and was able to recognize him when he appeared, she could say, "Thank you for your suggestion, King Ed," and then override his commands if she found them pompous.

Remember that no subpersonality is "all of you." You can always talk to her, reason with her, listen to her, and then decide what you want to do. No subpersonality—not even a heroic one—can dominate. You're the boss.

Lois was immensely relieved to find that "Loved-Starved Linda" was only a part of her personality, not all of her. She began to understand that this subpersonality—and *only* this part of her—needed an overabundance of attention and affection. She could now talk to and comfort this needy side of herself, which had lost the power to dominate her.

DEVELOPING TRAITS YOU WANT

Now that you are aware of some of your major personality traits, you can begin to work on those that need strengthening—and you can also create traits that you want.

Is there any new subpersonality you would like to have? The following list of characters may give you some ideas.

King

Lady

Inner Child

Adventurer

Heroine

Genius

Spiritual Guide

Warrior

Critic

Sensualist

Artist

Again, envision the trait you would like to develop. What does it look like?

_____

_____

List the desirable qualities you would like to develop. Now give each a character and a name, and recite the phrase "I am _____" (filling in the name of each subpersonality—for example, "Brave Joan").

Visualize a situation that requires this trait. For example, let's say you are working on courage. Imagine asking a friend for a favor, or asking your boss for a raise. Visualize your brave subpersonality fusing intimately with your center. Become aware of the particular emotions that the image elicits, and stay with this image for a while. Now you can call on this subpersonality whenever you wish.

Now, create a situation in your life in which you can exercise your new subpersonality. Let it be something simple. If, for instance, you experience fear when dealing with your boss or another colleague, start with the colleague. Try to choose a "no-lose" situation—for example, a time when you feel the evidence is on your side. Recite to yourself the phrase, "I am (name of subpersonality)," and summon the accompanying mental image. You are now ready to deal with that colleague.

We can never control the results of a confrontation, but there is healing simply in allowing new aspects of our personalities to come forth.

HOW YOUR INNER SELVES INTERACT

Together, your subpersonalities act like a committee inside your mind. Sometimes they agree with one another; at other times they disagree violently.

How do your various subpersonalities interact? Does any one aspect of your personality bully or override another? The next exercise will help you to discover how your subpersonalities interact and how you can resolve conflicts among them.

On a separate sheet of paper, write the names of your subpersonalities in a circle shape, as illustrated. Draw arrows between your warring subpersonality parts. If one part dominates another, draw an arrow from the dominator to the dominated part.

King

Lady   Heroine

Inner Child   Genius

Adventurer   Warrior

Spiritual Guide   Critic

Artist   Sensualist

One thirty-year-old woman found that her subpersonalities "Critic" and "Adventurer" were in conflict. A tour guide, she could indulge her dream of seeing the world. But the Critic nagged at her to settle down and have children. She was able to let her two voices talk and work out a compromise.

If there is a conflict between any of your various subpersonalities, set up a conversation between them. Let them talk to each other, and write down their responses.

_____

_____

_____

_____

MOVING TOWARD INTEGRATION

"I was being the one person I am, instead of playing different roles with different people."

ALICE KOLLER

As you become conscious of all of your subpersonalities, each will gain a place on the stage of your mind. Eventually, the conflicts among them will begin to be resolved, and you will experience a deepened sense of wholeness.

As you move toward personality integration, you will notice some of the following signs. Place a check mark next to any of these milestones that you have experienced:

_____ You can be yourself, no matter who walks into your living room or into your life. You no longer have to play the whining child with your parents or the temptress with a man.

_____ You can enjoy time with others as well as time alone.

_____ A romantic relationship no longer has the power to take over your life.

_____ Once you are involved in a romantic relationship, you continue your friendships and maintain your interests.

_____ While you may be upset if a relationship ends, you are not down for long. Your friends, interests, and private talks with yourself see you through rebuffs and contingencies.

_____ When you hear the voice of one of your partial selves, you listen to her. You accept and understand her. You can call up her opposite, integrating both voices into a new aspect of your personality.

The Turning Point: Ruth

Ruth is a healthy-looking woman of sixty-nine, with intense blue eyes and a halo of fluffy white hair. She has become a role model for many younger women in her Kansas City support group.

But Ruth was not always a leader. Like many women who love too much, she was once a silent, submissive caretaker. She had followed the cultural script that encourages women to become half-persons. Often, a woman who is widowed or whose marriage ends after a long, traditional marriage is left with no skills for acting in the world. But when Ruth's husband died, she gave herself permission to develop other aspects of her personality and talents.

Ruth grew up during the Great Depression. When she was six, her father developed tuberculosis and left the family home to live in a sanitarium. Ruth's mother went to work to support the family. Ruth became the "little mother," cooking, cleaning, taking care of her brothers and sisters—and missing out on childhood.

When she was twenty-one, she married a handsome but sickly man named George, who reminded her of her father. George was an alcoholic. The couple had two sons, and Ruth continued the role she had learned in childhood.

During her thirty-nine-year marriage, Ruth remained quiet and submissive. The couple rarely spoke. George a salesman, knew only his sales pitch. Ruth had big ideas, but she never shared them. Still, when George developed inoperable cancer, she knew she would miss him terribly, and told him how she felt.

When George died, I had no regrets. We had stood by each other in good times and bad. But after the mourning, there came a turning point. What was I going to do? I realized that I did not have to be who I had always been. I knew I was a good homemaker, but all my friends were good homemakers. I asked myself, What do *I* have to offer that's unique?

I had always wanted to be a teacher. I have only a high-school education, but I had been keeping a journal for twenty-eight years. I approached the local community center with the idea of teaching a class in journal writing. They approved my course outline. I loved being a teacher. A few months later, the dean of humanities at Kansas State called me and said, "We've heard about you." They wanted me to teach at State! It gave me such a sense of self-worth.

I found out I was a good conversationalist and a catalyst, parts of me that I had never been aware of. I had always thought that I was flat and one-dimensional. But I began to realize that I was multifaceted, like a diamond. I thought, "If I can get that part of me to shine, why not try another?"

I realized that I wanted to make more friends, so I joined organizations and extended myself. I began to count on my women friends, which I had never done before. One young friend would pick me up in her red sports car to go disco dancing! I was pretty close to sixty, but I felt about eighteen. I had lost the child in me very early, but now I rediscovered that blithe spirit.

I spent many years without a lover, developing myself and my friendships. When I met a man who interested me in one of my classes, I was shocked to see his apartment. It was total chaos. I had the strongest urge to clean up the mess. Instead of falling back into that old role, I suggested we spend the weekend at my place. Now that I have a very full life, my sense of self does not depend on taking care of anyone else.

CHAPTER 7

Defining Your Boundaries

> " I'm learning where I start and where I end. I'm learning how much I can yield to people I dislike and how much I can yield to those I love. "

SHARON

Our personal boundaries influence how we feel about ourselves and how we relate to everyone else. We are not usually aware on a conscious level that such boundaries exist—but if we ever feel that someone is getting too close and crowding us, either psychologically or physically, or withdrawing and becoming distant, we quickly become aware of these boundaries. Boundaries represent the psychological dividing lines between us and other people.

Boundaries are important because they allow us to maintain a healthy sense of self as an individual, separate from everyone and everything else. This sense of identity is something that children from functional families learn very early. Without this sense, you cannot achieve balance or maintain your own values and goals while encountering the influences and emotions of others.

For the typical woman who loves too much, blurred boundaries are generally the result of having grown up in a family in which personal boundaries were either unclear or nonexistent.

Perhaps we were told, either explicitly or implicitly, "We are a family—one unit that is more important than its individual members." Or we may have been led to believe that our feelings should always reflect those of a parent. Perhaps the boundaries between us and other family members were blurred by invasive behavior, such as lack of privacy or physical, emotional, or sexual abuse. Where individuality is not respected, boundaries do not exist. Thus, it may never have been clear to us whose feelings we were actually experiencing.

Often, those who love others excessively or addictively have weak or blurred personal boundaries. Such a person feels merged with her partner, experiencing the sensation that she and the partner "are one." It almost seems as though the other person were living inside her skin.

Psychologists call this need to merge "symbiosis" or "projective identification." When it occurs, the other person's feelings typically seem more real to us than our own. We become so consumed with that person's concerns and problems that we lose your own direction, as well as our sense of self.

When we learn how to build better personal boundaries, our relationships improve. In fact, we cannot have healthy intimacy without healthy boundaries. If we don't know which emotions are ours and which are our partner's, or if we think that his opinions are always right, we are unable to hear the messages that our minds and bodies are sending us about what is true for us and what is not. To be healthy, we must know our own feelings and our own opinions.

An unhealthy person is not capable of a healthy relationship. Houston therapist John Bradshaw believes that having good boundaries is the most important factor in intimacy. Says Bradshaw, "Only when we have good boundaries can we expand our boundaries with someone else. Only when we have strong boundaries can we love."

TROUBLE WITH BOUNDARIES IN THE PAST

> " When my mother was around, my father didn't own his own bedroom slippers. "
>
> CHRIS

In adulthood, damaged boundaries can lead you to believe that you have no right to privacy or private time and no right to say no. This impairs your ability to be intimate in a healthy way. The following exercise can help you to see whether your personal boundaries have been damaged—the first step in establishing healthy boundaries.

In childhood, did you ever feel as if you were merging into someone else, as if two of you had become one? Did you ever hear your mother or father say something like "I'm tired—go to bed"?

_____

_____

Was this feeling of merged identities pleasant or unpleasant for you?

_____

_____

When you were a child, did anyone refuse to respect your privacy? (For example, did anyone read your mail or refuse to let you be alone, even in the bathroom?)

_____

_____

Was there one person in your family who got to trample on everyone else's boundaries?

_____

_____

Did someone in your family always presume to know how you thought or felt?

_____

_____

Did your parents deny you the right to be an individual because they felt the family as a whole was more important than any one member?

_____

_____

When you first attempted to leave home or separate from your family, did they continue to interfere with your actions and decisions?

_____

_____

ASSESSING YOUR BOUNDARIES TODAY

> " I know a woman is going to make it when she can stand her own ground. "
>
> EDITH FREEMAN (PSYCHOTHERAPIST)

Doing this exercise will help you to see whether your boundaries are still unclear.

With a close friend or lover, do you ever feel as if you are merging into someone else, as if the two of you had become one? (For example, do you ever think, "If he likes the movie, then I like the movie?")

_____

_____

Is this feeling of merged identities pleasant or unpleasant for you?

_____

_____

In adulthood, does anyone in your life force his or her opinions or feelings on you? With whom do you have to constantly set limits?

_____

_____

In a relationship, do you ever blame yourself for someone else's problem? ("He can't commit. It must be my fault.")

_____

_____

In a romantic relationship, does your lover insist that you have sex whether you want to or not?

_____

_____

Do you have control over the money you earn, or does your lover? Do you choose the clothes you buy, or are they imposed on you by someone else?

_____

_____

If you have children, do you find it difficult to say no to them, and, when it's important, to put your own priorities first?

_____

_____

You can begin to reclaim and clarify your boundaries by learning to establish limits. There are times when it is appropriate to say, "This behavior is okay with me, but this other behavior is not okay." There are also times when you may want to say, "I'll think about it" or "Absolutely not." There are times when words are ineffective, and setting limits means walking out the door or taking the time to meet your own needs rather than the demands of another person.

Even when you have made enormous gains in your recovery, there will still be people and situations that will challenge your new sense of self. Even with stronger boundaries, there is still the possibility—even the probability—that you will lose yourself now and then. When this happens, don't panic or criticize yourself. It's all right to lose yourself from time to time, as long as you know how to get yourself back.

The following exercise will enable you to clarify your own boundaries as you interact with others and to restore yourself after losing them.

Losing Yourself

Before you can begin to restore lost personal boundaries, you first need to know how and in what ways you are currently letting your boundaries be overwhelmed by others. Place a check mark by any phrase that describes what losing yourself feels like for you. Place two checks next to the kind of loss that is most painful for you.

_____ You ignore your own feelings, while feeling someone else's feelings very intensely.

_____ You rescue someone with no thought of your own safety and well-being.

_____ You take orders from someone who is telling you what to do, even when you know that the action you're taking as a result is not the best one for you.

_____ You pretend that your opinions and interests match someone else's, when in fact they differ.

_____ You become sexually involved with someone before you are ready, just to please him.

_____ You accept the other person's point of view while discounting your own.

_____ You feel someone else's pain before you feel your own.

_____ You change your plans at the last minute to suit the whims of a new lover.

_____ You give endlessly of your time, talents, money, and services.

_____ You blame yourself for someone else's drunkenness, rudeness, thoughtlessness, or irresponsibility.

Restoring Your Boundaries

When you begin to feel a blurring of your boundaries with those of others, you need to raise your awareness of your own physical and emotional boundaries as ending at your own skin. This exercise can help you to regain your balance when you experience one of the above losses.

First, take a deep breath. Now touch your face with your fingertips. Ask yourself, "What are my feelings right now?" Acknowledge whether you are feeling fear, guilt, anger, joy, compassion, or the weight of responsibility. Then ask yourself, "Is there anything I need to do to reestablish my boundaries now?" Follow your own answer.

What follows are some techniques for recontacting your sense of identity:

- Stay with your feeling. Give yourself permission to feel it fully. (Do not cross over to what you believe the other person is feeling.)

- Express your feeling out loud, perhaps sharing it with someone else. You deserve to say how you feel.

- State your preference (for example, "I'd rather not go into that right now" or "I would like to go to that restaurant instead"). This helps you to maintain clarity about your own choices and priorities.

- Set limits ("I can help you do this, but I can't help you do that"). These limits will help you give to others within healthy boundaries, so that you don't overextend yourself.

- Disagree. Acknowledge the other person's opinion and restate your own. When you air your differences, you will not resort to pretending or accommodating in order to keep the peace.

- Talk about your own experience, such as how you handled such an incident, rather than how the other person should do it.

- Use the word *you* in a sentence to remind yourself that this is the other person's problem (for example, "You really didn't need that on top of everything else").

- Hand the problem back to its originator. Acknowledge the difficulty of the problem, then give the person the freedom to solve his or her own problem ("That's really a tough one, but I'm sure you'll be able to figure it out.")

Quickly sorting through your options like this takes practice, but the payoff can be tremendous. You will have reestablished your boundaries. You will no longer carry the weight of someone else's problems and responsibilities. You will be back in your own body, taking care of yourself, with a strong sense of who you are and where you are going.

If you have lost yourself in a more serious or long-term way (typically, by becoming completely merged with someone in an intimate relationship), you may have come to a startling realization: "I don't know who I am anymore." When this painful loss of one's sense of identity occurs because of addictive love, it can be a frightening, rude awakening—particularly if the relationship ends abruptly.

Despite the pain of such a situation, there are ways in which you can utilize your natural abilities to recover and restore your personal boundaries. Recovering your boundaries does not take new abilities; instead, it draws on skills that you already possess. Your knowledge of what actions were most helpful—and least helpful—for you in the past can be very helpful to you. The following exercise will help you to become conscious of the skills you already have that you can use to restore yourself after such a loss of self:

Describe an incident, relationship, or long-term situation in which you felt you had lost yourself.

_____

_____

_____

What actions helped you to regain your sense of self? (for example, calling a friend, telling someone that you had changed your mind, going for a walk, having a talk with your inner child, praying or meditating, writing an angry but unsent letter, going to an Al-Anon meeting)

_____

_____

_____

After this loss of self, which of your actions did you find least helpful? (for example, mentally beating yourself up, immediately searching for a new man, eating a lot of sweets, shopping compulsively)

_____

_____

_____

PREVENTING THE LOSS OF SELF

Some people fear that in order to prevent losing themselves, they must avoid romantic relationships altogether. Fortunately, this is not true. You can learn to maintain healthy boundaries that will remain whether or not you are in a relationship.

As you progress in your recovery, you will be able to strengthen your sense of self and reinforce your boundaries by focusing your attention on nurturing yourself. Several daily activities can help to keep you on an even keel. In my support group, we made a list of the activities we use to bring ourselves into balance, dividing the list by time of day and frequency.

One woman's list read like this:

Morning
Meditation

Noon
Exercise
Frequent work breaks

Evening
Dancing
Playtime
Speak with friends

Once a Week
Movies
Art exhibit
Therapist
Take my inner child on a field trip

What would your ideal list be like?

CLARIFYING PERSONAL BOUNDARIES

> "A nice guy won't punish you for setting limits.
> He wants the best for you."
>
> ROBIN NORWOOD

Now that you know how to restore and maintain your own personal boundaries after losing your sense of identity, you can begin the work of exploring and clarifying the boundaries that exist between you and others. When you are not used to seeing these limits, they can be hard to grasp at first. It is probably difficult even to realize that there *is* any difference between you and someone you love intensely, anyplace where a boundary could be drawn. The first step in defining your personal boundaries, then, is learning to perceive the differences between you and those you love.

When you become so merged with someone that you have lost your sense of self and feel that the other person's feelings and actions are your own, you inevitably end up thinking that you are responsible for his actions—abuse, alcoholism, affairs, depression, or criminal activity—and that these actions reflect some failing or flaw in you. In order to recover your lost sense of identity as a separate self, you need to realize that you are not responsible for anyone else's actions, or even for their reactions to your actions. They alone are responsible for their actions and reactions.

This exercise will help you to more clearly define the boundaries between you and others.

If a friend promises to call and does not call, what does this say about you?

_____

_____

_____

What does it say about your friend?

_____

_____

_____

If a man can't make commitments, what does that say about you?

_____

_____

_____

What does that say about him?

_____

_____

_____

If someone close to you drinks too much, what does that say about you?

_____

_____

_____

What does that say about the other person?

_____

_____

_____

If a friend is verbally abusive, what does that say about you?

_____

_____

_____

What does it say about your friend?

_____

_____

_____

If you have to put on a false self in order to spend time with a person, what does that say about you?

_____

_____

_____

What does that say about the other person?

_____

_____

_____

If a man cannot love, what does that say about you?

_____

_____

_____

What does that say about him?

_____

_____

_____

SETTING BOUNDARIES

> **"**I feel strong enough to ask for the help I need.**"**
>
> ROKELLE LERNER

When you begin to realize that the actions and reactions of others are not caused by you, that you are a separate person and that everyone else is, too, you will have a solid basis on which to define your own personal boundaries. These boundaries represent the limits to which we feel comfortable in various situations. Most women who love too much do not think to object or to refuse to participate when someone they love wants them to do something they don't want to do.

If the idea of asking to have things the way you want them is a new one to you, you may feel uncomfortable with the idea and even afraid to try it at first. If that is the case, try practicing this next exercise in your imagination for a while. Then take the plunge and put it into practice in your recovery group or with a close friend with whom you feel safe. After that, slowly work your way through increasingly difficult situations. Once you have made a beginning, you will be surprised at how easy it becomes.

Say each of these sentences out loud, imagining the intended listener:

(To a department-store clerk) "I'll need the beds delivered by Tuesday at the latest."

(To a friend) "I lent you $500 in January. I'd like it back by the end of May."

(To your brother) "By all means, bring Matthew to the picnic, but the party that night is for adults only."

(To a new lover) "I love you, but I can't come over tonight. I have to work."

Which, if any, was difficult for you to say?

_____

_____

_____

What feeling came up when you said this? (for example, guilt, compassion, resentment, anger)

_____

_____

Is there an emotional trigger from your past that makes it difficult for you to set limits? (You could not say no to your father.)

_____

_____

What advantages do you think you gain from setting these limits? (increased self-esteem, establishing boundaries, respecting your needs, etc.)

_____

_____

_____

What are the disadvantages of setting limits? (possibly inconveniencing someone, surprising someone who thinks he or she knows you, possible rejection, making waves)

_____

_____

_____

SETTING LIMITS ON GIVING

> " Women who love too much are women who give too much. "

NORA

Women who have trouble defining boundaries between themselves and others tend to get caught in a cycle of overgiving. Feeling needy themselves, they give continually to others, hoping in this way to meet their own needs. When their generosity is not met with the gratefulness they feel they deserve, they may decide that the problem is that they are not giving *enough,* and they proceed to give even more.

Generosity is a healthy human instinct, but when it is all one-sided it becomes unhealthy. You may have spent hours on the phone listening to the problems of friends, lovers, or relatives. You may have overgiven in money, sex, time, or affection, and you may often have wondered why others didn't give to you as you had given to them.

You can learn to give without giving yourself away. This exercise will help you to begin to see how to give enough to others while still giving enough to yourself.

Say each of these sentences out loud, imagining the intended listener:

(To a charitable organization) "I can't make a large contribution right now, but here is ten dollars."

(To a friend) "I can spend the morning helping you clean, but not the afternoon."

(To your sister) "I'm not willing to cook the entire Thanksgiving dinner, like I usually do, but I'll be happy to bring my famous pecan pie."

(To a new love interest) "Now I'd like to tell you what happened to *me* today."

Which, if any, was difficult for you to say?

_____

_____

What feeling came up when you said this? (for example, guilt, compassion, resentment, anger)

_____

_____

Is there an emotional trigger from your past that makes it difficult for you to set limits on giving? (Perhaps as a child you were expected to care for your sick brother.)

_____

_____

_____

What are the advantages of setting limits on giving? (increased self-esteem, establishing boundaries, respecting your needs, etc.)

_____

_____

_____

What are the disadvantages of setting limits on giving? (possibly inconveniencing someone, surprising someone who thinks they know you, possible rejection, making waves)

_____

_____

_____

PROGRESS IN STRENGTHENING

You can tell you are beginning to strengthen your boundaries when (check any breakthrough you have already experienced):

_____ You act on feelings when you need to.

_____ You can say no when you want to without experiencing tidal waves of guilt.

_____ You generally do precisely what you want to do rather than depending on the suggestions of others.

_____ You no longer blame yourself for everything that goes wrong in a relationship or friendship.

_____ You no longer feel responsible for making a relationship work or making another person happy.

_____ You don't take things so personally. If a friend is inconsiderate or a partner has a wandering eye, you know the action may have come from that person's history.

_____ You disagree with a friend and yet are able to maintain your friendship.

_____ You realize that you are not responsible for the actions of another.

_____ You become comfortable in receiving as well as giving.

The Turning Point: Shelley

Shelley, thirty-nine, is a recovering alcoholic. She is tall, with wheat-colored hair and a glow to her cheeks. She looks as though she runs several miles every morning—which she does. She lives in Denver, where she has started a software-marketing company.

Shelley grew up in a family in which there was an unhealthy lack of boundaries. She says that her parents "pretended they lived in the same skin." They never disagreed, never argued, and never expressed any negative emotions. Shelley learned that "if you were in love, you were forever merged with someone in a sense of total oneness."

In Shelley's adult life, if her boyfriend, Jack, did something she did not like, she did not bring up the subject for fear of losing him. She finally broke up with Jack. After having spent six months alone, Shelley found that she could disagree with her new lover, Paul, without fear of abandonment.

When I joined an independent Women Who Love Too Much group, I could see clearly that I was contorting myself to stay with Jack, no matter what. He was dating another woman; he would show up late or not at all; he would not want to make love, or he'd be disinterested if we did make love. Instead of discussing any of these problems with him or standing up for myself, I'd try to be prettier or funnier or more understanding, believing that if I were different, I could control the situation.

I could see that I was selling out my soul to be with him. I was so afraid of any conflict, afraid that if there were any differences between us he would abandon me. Finally, I could see that the man I wanted to be prettier and funnier and more understanding for did not want to be in a relationship with me.

Three days before Christmas, I broke up with Jack, which was very tough. The old me would have tried to patch things together until January. My mode would have been to then quickly find a replacement for him, a "back-pocket" man.

I barely made it through Christmas, and by New Year's I

was really at a low. But I sat with the ache and didn't try to drug my way out, so it turned into growth. My willingness for the first time to be alone without a replacement, at an inconvenient time, was a real help to me. My turning point in recovery came during that six months when I let myself be alone and really came to grips with the fact that I might very well spend my life without a lover.

As I continued to go to my groups, I grew less desperate to merge with someone. I spent a lot of time with men, but I think I was putting out some sort of subconscious vibes that told potential lovers: "I need time to heal."

I noticed I was on the road to health when my current relationship started, because it began differently from any relationship I'd ever had. I was not initially attracted to Paul. He was cute, but not my type. I had always been attracted to the classic starving-poet type. Paul was very straight-looking, and he wasn't needy. We saw each other for a month, and at the end of each date we shook hands at the door. I did not want to sleep with him right away. Because I didn't feel invested, I could be free to look at his actions and mine.

And I was beginning to break out of my family's message that "we are all one, and everything is fine." I began to feel a sense of separateness. I was telling Paul what the truth was for me. I found that if I wanted to disagree with him or ask for something from him, I could not look at his face. If I did look in his eyes, I would notice whether or not I got approval, and I would adjust my feelings or opinions accordingly. So we devised a way to sit side by side in a restaurant. That way I could tell him, "When you said that, I felt hurt," and so forth, without adjusting myself to agree with him.

I asked him anything I wanted to know. By the time we kissed each other, we had already discussed the fact that I didn't need to have children and that he was willing to get married (though not necessarily to me) again, even though he was coming out of a bad marriage.

I needed to go slowly, and I needed to say who I was, to present myself, all along the way. Paul was willing to go slowly, too. He actually told me that he had never learned about intimacy and wanted to learn what it was. I'm afraid I was a bit of a chauvinist. I didn't believe such a good man existed. I thought it was a woman's role to want a relationship and a man's role to avoid it.

We did not agree on everything. After seven months, I wanted to commit myself to him. It was only after a year that he wanted that very much, too. We have been married now for seven months. On occasion, I still have the strong urge to merge with him, but I am starting to be more comfortable with disagreement.

I did not say, "I have a boundary issue, and I don't want to merge with you." I was not yet aware of those words. It was just that I was on a health-oriented path. There was a gradual sense of self-acceptance and a willingness to be myself in the presence of Paul, whether we agreed on everything or not.

Finding Spirituality

" "Our inner state of mind determines our outer life, not the other way around. **" "**

JACQUELYN SMALL

If you have tried to break an addictive habit—such as cigarette smoking or overeating—through willpower alone, you have probably realized the immense difficulty of the struggle. Just saying no is not enough, because this superficial strategy does not reach down to the cause of the craving.

As long as we engage in hand-to-hand combat with the addiction, we maintain the struggle, and the addiction wins. Ironically, however, the moment we stop the contest and acknowledge our powerlessness, we find a deeper power.

Admitting "weakness" is almost always socially unacceptable in Western culture. However, for those recovering from addictive love, it is essential to make this admission—to surrender. Surrendering is very different from merely submitting to the situation. In the book of daily thoughts *One Day at a Time in Al-Anon,* Harry M. Tiebout discusses the difference between surrender and submission:

> In submission, an individual accepts reality consciously but not unconsciously. There is always a feeling lurking in the back of your unconscious mind, that "there will come a day" . . . the assumption that magically the problem will, one fine day, just disappear.

If this is how we feel, we are only submitting. Tiebout says this means that we have not accepted the problem on a deep level, and our internal struggle continues with an underlying current of tension. However, he says, when we fully surrender, "there is no residual battle. There is relaxation and freedom from strain and conflict." It is in surrender that we find recovery and gain the grace of acceptance that Tiebout calls "a state of mind in which the individual accepts, rather than rejects or resists; he (or she) is able to take things in, to go along with, to cooperate and be receptive."

As unlikely as it may seem, our acceptance of some measure of powerlessness can be a very positive thing. If we accept the premise that we are powerless over our obsessions, our feelings, someone else's behavior, or our own behavior at times, then we need not exhaust ourselves in trying to seek solutions or control the results. We need only surrender—and we will be free of the burden. We will be able to seek help and to ask for support from others. Paradoxically, by admitting some lack of power, you will be able to lead yourself to a calm, healing place.

Another concept, one that is closely related to the idea of surrender, concerns letting go of the illusion that we can conquer the problem if only we can muster sufficient willpower. According to one psychologist, "No one ever got out of an addiction by willing his way out of it."

If we are addicted to love, we are probably accustomed to trying harder. We have worked hard to make our relationships succeed; we have worked on ourselves in an effort to become perfect; and we have tried to change our lovers into our fantasy images of how we want them to be.

To recover from addictive love, we do not have to struggle to "fix" anything or anyone. Instead of giving so much to others and striving to save the day, we can receive love and support. We do not have to work so hard. We can just be.

FINDING YOUR HIGHER POWER

> " The specific meaning of God depends on what is the most desirable good for a person. "
>
> ERICH FROMM

Several of the women interviewed for this book talked about the void they felt inside. Many of us have tried unsuccessfully to fill our personal emptiness with drugs, alcohol, men, sex, or work. For a long time, our addictions let us run away from the pain; sometimes they gave us a false sense of courage. But none of our addictions filled the void or brought us peace. If you are a woman who loves too much, the void or emptiness you feel inside is caused not by the lack of another person or a lack of intimacy, but by a lack of contact with your deeper self.

When you can surrender to what is and begin to let go of struggling, you will discover a source of power that can help to speed your recovery. This source goes by many names, but it is most often referred to in Twelve-Step programs as a Higher Power or Higher Self. Finding your Higher Power means finding a deep inner source of well-being. Some people call this feeling spirituality. Spirituality can range from being at one with living things to believing that there is a Higher Power who guides you.

Some people find it easier to think about their Higher Power as something that exists outside them. If you are not comfortable with thinking of your Higher Power in religious terms, you may wish to place your trust in the loveliness of nature or in the safety and strength of your recovery group. Others conceive of their Higher Power as an inner, wiser part of themselves. You can choose the power in which you place your trust.

What can your Higher Power or Higher Self do for you? Human relationships are at best uncertain: a lover can leave, parents can disapprove and withdraw love, friends can move away or abandon us through death. Many of us have made a man (a father, husband, or lover) into a kind of Higher Power, only to feel abandoned when the relationship has ended. When we place our trust in a true Higher Power, however, we can have a deeper, unending source of strength. By relying on your Higher Power, you will be able to say no to your addiction. You will experience daily ups and downs in a new way. You will learn to find real meaning in life, and to connect to the best in yourself and the best in others.

For many of us, belief in a Higher Power or Higher Self does not come easily. Awakening to this belief is a slow, subtle process. The turning point at this stage typically comes when you are at a crossroads, faced with a problem that you don't know how to deal with. Instead of asking a friend—or ten friends—to solve the problem for you, you turn to your source, your inner power.

What do you believe in? Take a moment to look within and find the terms that come closest to your beliefs at this time. Name this source here:

_____

_____

The following exercises can help you to find the source of your Higher Power.

PRAYER

> **"** Explore daily the will of God. **"**
>
> C. G. JUNG

Prayer is one tool for communicating with your Higher Power or Higher Self. Prayer is simply talking to your Higher Power. When you are intimate with someone, you feel free to express your feelings. When you are intimate with your Higher Power, you feel free to say that you are happy, sad, grateful, or in need.

My prayers are like little chats, like telling a trusted friend my thoughts and feelings. I ask for wisdom and strength, and I thank my Higher Power for the gifts in my life.

Write your prayer here:

_____

_____

_____

_____

_____

_____

_____

A Way to Pray

If you are at a loss for words, here is an aid for talking to your Higher Power or Higher Self.

I see you today in _____ (my child, my friend, my lover, my parent, myself, in some aspect of nature).

I am feeling _____ right now because my lover said or did _____.

I felt your presence today in myself when I _____.

The new understanding that has come to me today is

_____.

Please help me let go of my attachment to _____.

Please help me to know whether to end my relationship with _____.

Sometimes I take _____ for granted, but today I am grateful for _____.

I feel a difficulty right now that is beyond me. I need your guidance and wisdom regarding _____.

Help me to see the _____ part of me that has been

dormant for too long.

Support me when I need to say no to _____ about

_____.

Please let me know what I can do today to improve my

relationship with _____.

MEDITATION

> " I used to have to force myself to meditate. Now it's the best part of my day. "

CHRISTINA

If prayer is talking to our Higher Power or Higher Self, meditation is listening. It is simply clearing our minds to hear the voice of our Higher Power speaking to us. With regard to meditation, Erich Fromm says that "the important thing is to step back from the bustle of life, to come to ourselves, to stop reacting to stimuli, to make ourselves empty so we can become active within ourselves."

The inner voice of our Higher Power is probably not as audible as that of our critical inner voices. To receive its guidance, we have to listen. Only when we have stilled the noise, both external and internal, can we hear the voice of the Higher Self.

There are many ways to meditate. You can take formal classes, read books, buy guided-meditation tapes, or simply sit in a comfortable chair, breathing quietly and regularly as you empty your mind.

When you begin to meditate, you may at first be aware of angry, chattering voices in your head constantly repeating negative messages—"You can't do it. Why even try?" But with practice, you'll be able to turn these voices down low enough to clear your mind for meditation, and eventually you'll be able to still them completely.

A Way to Meditate

In *The Meditative Mind,* Daniel Goleman provides the following simple instructions for how to meditate:

> Find a comfortable, straight-back chair in a quiet room, where you will not be disturbed. Sit up straight but relaxed. Keep your head, neck, and spine aligned, as though a large helium balloon was lifting your head up. Keeping your head upright will help your mind stay more alert—and alertness is essential in meditation.
>
> Close your eyes, and keep them closed until the session has ended. It's best to sit for at least fifteen minutes at a time, preferably longer—twenty or thirty minutes, or even an hour, if possible. You should decide how long you will meditate before you begin. That way you won't yield so easily to the temptation to get up and do something "more useful." Urges to stop meditating will come and go, and you should resist them. Set a timer or peek at your watch from time to time to see if the session is over.
>
> One of the simplest practices is meditation on the breath. Although it was the method that reportedly brought the Buddha to enlightenment, it has also found a more mundane use in psychotherapy and behavioral medicine as a technique for becoming deeply relaxed.
>
> To begin, bring your awareness to your breath, noticing each inhalation and exhalation. You can watch the breath either by feeling the sensations at the nostrils or by noting the rise and fall of your belly as you breathe.
>
> Try to be aware of each breath for its full duration—the entire in-breath. Do not try to control your breath; just watch it. If your breathing gets more shallow, let it be shallow. If it gets faster or slower, let it. The breath regulates itself. While you meditate, your job is simply to be aware of it.
>
> Whenever you notice that your mind has wandered, gently

bring it back to your breath. During meditation, you need to view everything other than your breath—thoughts, plans, memories, sounds, sensations—as distractions. Let go of your other thoughts. Whatever comes into your mind besides your breath is, for now, not to be heeded.

If you have trouble keeping your mind on your breath, you can help maintain your focus by repeating a word with each inhalation and exhalation. If you are watching your breath at the nostrils, think "in" with each inhalation, "out" with each exhalation. If you are watching the rise and fall of your belly, think "rising" with each inhalation, "falling" with each exhalation. Be sure to stay in touch with the actual experience of breathing, not merely the repetition of the words.

Whatever method you use, meditation can help you to clear your mind so that you can listen to a spiritual voice from within.

TURNING IT OVER

> "I just do the footwork and leave the results to God."
>
> MARIANNE

Once you are in contact with your Higher Power, you can turn to it whenever you are in need of guidance. There are times when we do not know the answers to our most pressing questions. We may become too confused to make the best decisions, such as whether to separate or to try to work out a relationship. By "turning it over" to a Higher Power, we are admitting that while we have the responsibility for our lives, we don't know what direction to take.

Trying to control our relationships can cause us to feel totally out of control in our lives. Paradoxically, when we give up trying to control the uncontrollable, we gain more power over that which is actually controllable—our choices.

It is wise to turn over to your Higher Power any problem with which you feel powerless. We are all powerless over results. When we interview for a job, we are powerless over the outcome. When we are in a love relationship, we are powerless over what will happen.

When we understand our powerlessness over the outcome of relationships, we are freed from carrying the entire responsibility for them. Instead of forcing an outcome, we can turn it over. Accepting our powerlessness means that we can stop our worry, anxiety, and obsession over a relationship.

If you find it difficult to let go and turn your problems over to your Higher Power, the following exercise may be of help.

Create a box to contain the wisdom of your Higher Power or Higher Self. You can decorate a shoe box or index-card file box with anything that, to you, symbolizes universal wisdom (for example, a Buddha, a cross, a Star of David, or a moon and stars).

Then think about what is troubling you—the need to find a new apartment, a problem at work, your current love relationship—anything over which you feel powerless. Write it on a piece of paper and place it in the box to symbolize your letting go of the problem and turning it over to your Higher Power. Now tell yourself that you no longer need to worry about or be obsessed by it.

Within a few hours, days, or weeks, you will find either that the problem has been resolved, perhaps through a surprising change in circumstances, or that you know precisely what steps to take to resolve it. The answer may have come to you in a dream or as an inspiration or an image during meditation.

For example, if you turned over your job, you might find that through an unforeseen series of events, you now have a new one. If you turned over your relationship, the answer from your Higher Power might be to enjoy your lover's friendship but to detach from any possessiveness over him and to expand your social contacts. Your answer to your work dilemma might have come in a dream in which you saw yourself living in a house by an ocean that continually rose up, shaking the foundations and washing into the house. This may have symbolized your knowledge that work has overtaken your life, and that you need to set limits on your working hours to regain your balance.

Remain open to whatever answer comes up, and don't be surprised if it's not the one you expected.

SERENITY: LIVING IN THE NOW

> **"** I don't take it one day at a time. I take it one *minute* at a time. **"**
>
> JOAN

In order to let go of outcomes, we need to let go of our concerns about the past and the future. We must learn to live in the present. The following is a powerful exercise designed to help you live in the moment.

Whenever you find your mind wandering to the past or projecting into the future, *stop.* Then ask yourself,

Right now, what do I hear, see, smell, taste, or touch?

_____

_____

What year is this?

_____

_____

What day is this?

_____

_____

What time is this?

_____

_____

Where am I?

_____

_____

Who am I with?

_____

_____

Who am I?

_____

_____

What am I feeling?

_____

_____

With practice, you can go quickly through this series of questions and bring yourself back to your current experience after any distraction.

DEVELOPING AN INNER LIFE

You will know that spiritual awakening is starting in your life when (check any that apply):

_____ You notice that you feel relaxed and at peace more often than you feel that familiar clenched-fist tightness.

_____ You stop manipulating others and trust that they can take care of themselves.

_____ You can turn to your Higher Power for advice any time you want.

_____ More often, you know intuitively what is important to you and what is not.

_____ You feel less helpless and less overwhelmed.

_____ You don't need to be with your lover every moment.

_____ You choose meditation over such distractions as compulsive television-watching or overeating.

_____ You no longer feel lonely simply because there is no one with you.

_____ You feel okay about yourself even when someone is angry with you.

_____ You see that you are imperfect, yet you know that you're worthwhile.

The Turning Point: Helen

Helen, thirty-six, is of medium height and is slight in build, with long, straight, shiny, auburn hair. She is an architect and a pet-lover—when interviewed, she was carrying a small white mouse on her shoulder.

For five years, Helen had been in a marriage that was a typical addictive-love relationship. She sums it up by saying, "He was very needy, and I was very controlling."

As an adult child of two alcoholic parents, Helen found it difficult to give up control. Eventually, however, she joined an ACA group and decided to get a divorce and start a new life. After several years in recovery, she had learned to "turn over" her love life to a Higher Power. Helen is now enjoying her first healthy relationship.

Ever since I can remember, I've believed in a power greater than myself. This was my loving parent, who gave me all the things my parents could never give me. After working in Twelve-Step programs for three and a half years, I've enlarged my view and have an even deeper feeling for my Higher Power.

My Higher Power became my lover, whom I love, who loves me, and who teaches me to receive love. I realized I had to develop a trust of my Higher Power before I could trust a human lover.

My Higher Power is also my guide. I had been turning over my life, *except* for my love life—the part that mattered most. I was afraid God would screw it up, or that he would say, "You have to be alone forever." I had many frustrating relationships.

A year ago, I turned over my love life. I said, "God, I give up. *You* find me someone." That was the turning point. It wasn't as if God said, "Here's the man for you," but I became more and more aware of what was going to work—or not going to work.

I met a man who was dating around to see if he really liked a woman he was seeing already. I told him I didn't like being involved in that, but I did not make him the bad guy. Then I met a nice man who was a workaholic. I told him I needed more than an occasional get-together. Again, I did not make him the villain. I met a man who was married. I decided I wanted more than a fantasy lover. Each involvement in an impossible relationship was getting shorter. One relationship lasted only a week, and one I did not get involved in at all.

In January, I started feeling friendlier toward everyone. At a reception, I met a man I liked but didn't feel romantically attracted to. My intuition about him was good, though, and we decided to go on a hike.

Kevin and I found that we had a lot in common. We're both architects. We both raised mice when we were kids. We like to hike at night, and we have many of the same friends. Six months after we met, Kevin moved into my place. This is the healthiest relationship I've ever had.

My need to control the relationship comes up again and again. But Kevin understands. His parents fought for dominance. Sometimes he can hear his mother's voice in me. When I recognize that I'm trying to control him, I'll say, "I'm sorry, I was getting snippy." I make amends. I'm willing to look at my own contribution to problems. But I stop short of taking his character inventory, and I don't demand that he make amends to me.

He's stubborn and won't go to ACA meetings, but he has a spiritual side. I find that if I want him to change, he resents it. But when he sees me change, he wants to change, too.

There are times when I get really rigid. When I hear myself

say, "It's my way or not at all," I turn over the problem again to my Higher Power. I say, "God, I can't help myself out of this. You can help me, and I'm going to let you." I get some surprising answers this way. It's like digging for buried treasure.

For instance, Kevin was spending most weeknights developing his photos in the darkroom. I wanted him to stop doing this so that we could spend more time together, but he had taken up photography and was enthusiastic. So one morning I turned over the problem to my Higher Power. The answer I received was, "Sometimes you can join him in the darkroom." So a couple of nights a week, we have a good time developing prints and talking. At other times I invite Kevin to share in some of my interests. Other nights I see my friends or work on painting. Little by little, I'm letting go of the need to change Kevin.

In my support groups I learned to develop some healthy selfishness. I did not feel I had to stay in a bad relationship out of loyalty. But at times, I've also had an unhealthy selfishness. Before I met Kevin, I wanted to be the star of a relationship. The script was ready, and I was looking for a supporting cast. In my relationship with Kevin we are equals, and no one is the star. Having a spiritual life has added something important to our relationship.

CHAPTER 9

Making New Choices

> " The healthier a person is, the more he or she is able to exercise choice, rather than compulsion. "

THEODORE ISAAC RUBIN

If you have faithfully made your way through the exercises in the earlier chapters of this book, you are likely beginning to experience a sense of the expanded possibilities you have and of the new and better choices you can make in your life. At first you may be hesitant, even frightened, at the thought of making new choices. You may even believe that you are not qualified or experienced enough to make decisions, particularly important ones.

Many of us grew up in dysfunctional homes in which we were allowed few choices. We may even have come to believe that we really have no choices. Our jobs seem to choose us, not the other way around. Lovers seem to choose us, not we them. Needy or abusive people seem to choose us.

But we are not actually without choices. Every day, we are choosing actively. The choices we make reflect our values, our worldviews, and our self-images. We inevitably choose what we think we deserve, and these choices shape our lives.

One of the most devastating effects of addictive love concerns loss of choice. We do not feel we have the right to choose.

We lose the ability to say no, to maintain our boundaries, to know what we believe, to remain in or to leave a relationship. If we are focused entirely on others, we accept their values and perspectives and fail to see alternatives that might enhance our lives.

When we are involved in relationships that are less than satisfying, an important turning point in our recovery occurs when we begin to see that we do have choices: we can remain, we can leave, or we can alter our relationship patterns. By acting on these choices, we can begin to become powerful in our own lives.

One trap to avoid at this stage of recovery is thinking that if we do what is good for us, such as leaving a relationship, we are going to hurt someone else. The reality is that by *not* doing what is good for us, we can also ultimately hurt someone else. If we remain in relationships in which we are miserable, our resentment and unhappiness will affect our partners. Giving ourselves new options means giving our partners new options as well.

At first, the idea of doing what's best for us may cause us to feel guilty or uncomfortable. This is because we have spent so many years convincing ourselves that we shouldn't put ourselves first. But if we persist in acting to fulfill our own needs, the feelings of guilt or discomfort will lessen. We can make the choices that are best for us without exploiting anyone else.

GIVING YOUR POWER AWAY

> " I do not wish them [women] to have power over men, but over themselves. "
>
> MARY WOLLSTONECRAFT

Many of us automatically give our power away without even realizing it. This exercise will help you to identify situations in which you have given your power of choice away. When you become conscious of the areas in which you are letting others make choices for you, you will begin to see that these are precisely the areas in which you could be exercising this power for yourself.

Fill in the blanks with your own experiences.

I have let _____ decide what I should

wear to _____.

I have let _____ decide where we should

eat lunch.

I have let _____ decide whether or not we

should make love.

I have let _____ decide on the evening's

entertainment.

I have let _____ decide who should drive.

List any other situations you can remember in which you recently let someone else make a decision for you. Do not be hard on yourself. Remember, awareness is the first step toward positive change.

MAKING DECISIONS

> **"** Today I will be conscious of all the little decisions I make, and I will accept all my decisions as right. **"**
>
> ROKELLE LERNER

Small Decisions: Everyday Awareness

If the thought of being powerful enough to make your own decisions seems a little hard to believe at the moment, recognizing the many small decisions you make every day is the first step toward making more important ones.

This exercise will help you to become aware of the choices you already make. Fill in the blanks.

Today, I decided to eat _____.

Today, I have decided that during the evening I will

_____.

This week, I decided I wanted to see the movie _____.

When _____ called and wanted to chat, I decided (to chat or not to chat) _____, and I let her know.

Today, I decided to spend _____ (amount of money) on

_____.

Today, I decided to (do or not do) _____ the housework.

List any other decisions you are aware of having made today.

Larger Decisions

Now that you are beginning to recognize the smaller decisions you have already made, it may help you to know that you also make larger ones—such as where to live, with whom to live, what kind of work to do, and whom to allow in your life. Some of these decisions you make consciously, others unconsciously.

Fill in the blanks below to discover what choices you have made, and continue to make, that shape your life.

I have decided to live in the _____ section of

_____ (city or town).

I have decided to live (alone, with my family, with a roommate, with a lover) _____.

I have decided to befriend _____ and to see what kind of relationship will develop.

I have decided to keep my present job at _____.

List any other important decisions you realize you have been making.

TAKING THE POWER YOU ALREADY HAVE

Now that you are beginning to see that you are constantly, if not consciously, making choices every day, the following checklist can help you to further identify those areas in which you are now exercising or not exercising your power of choice, and in which you sometimes exercise that power but could benefit from doing so more frequently.

Place a plus sign (+) next to any power you regularly exercise, a minus sign (−) next to any power you rarely exercise, and both a plus *and* a minus sign (+ −) next to those powers you sometimes use.

I have already taken:

_____ My power to change the subject of a conversation.

_____ My power to terminate a conversation.

_____ My power to end a destructive friendship or relationship.

_____ My power to indicate interest in someone and see what happens.

_____ My power to indicate disinterest in a romantic relationship but interest in a friendship.

_____ My power to leave if someone is abusing or humiliating me.

_____ My power to decide what I will do with my time.

_____ My power to choose what's important and what's not important to me, and to live by that.

_____ My power to say what I like and what I don't like.

_____ My power to proceed at whatever pace feels comfortable to me in a new relationship.

_____ My power to admit a truth to myself and, in a safe environment, to share some fact of that truth with others.

_____ My power to listen to others' advice, if I wish, but then to do what is best for me.

_____ My power to decide what I want in a relationship.

Do you see any areas in which you are not exercising your power of choice or in which you could be exercising it more fully? Next time the opportunity to take action in any of these areas occurs, be sure that your behavior comes from a conscious exercise of your own power to choose.

CHOOSING QUALITIES YOU WANT IN A PARTNER

> **"**Women receive ferocious training in the direction away from thinking, 'What do I want?' We tend to think far more in terms of 'What do they want (need) of me?'**"**
>
> DR. JUDITH BARDWICK
> (AS QUOTED BY MAGGIE SCARF)

Once we have acknowledged our power over our lives, the next step is to visualize clearly our goal. When we know what we want from our relationships, we can make our decisions accordingly.

One very important decision we make is to choose a man who has the capacity for a mutually nurturing relationship. What are the qualities of such a man?

The list compiled by the women in one group included the following:

Understanding

Monogamy

Trust

Affection

Intellectual stimulation

Compatibility

Nurturing

Empathy

Fun

Safety

Support

What are the elements you need in a relationship in order to feel loved, cherished, and respected? Make a list of the qualities you feel a nurturing partner should have.

CHOOSING TO LEAVE

> " Until you know how to get out of a relationship, you'll never be free to choose to stay in one. "
>
> TERENCE GORSKI

Relationships force you to make a wide range of choices, including deciding on the degree of intimacy you feel comfortable with and deciding whether to continue or end the relationship. Some of us flee at the first sign of a problem, and some of us stay in bad relationships beyond the limits of wisdom. To develop your capacity for making choices, you need to know when and how to leave a relationship responsibly. The following questions can help you to determine whether it is time to leave a relationship.

I tend to be someone who (flees, stays, makes wise choices)

_____.

When I think about leaving, I feel (guilt, resentment, anger, sadness, loss, relief) _____.

I would like to experiment in my relationships by (hanging in there longer, getting out sooner, making wiser choices in the first place) _____.

What I would miss about this relationship is _____.

What I would not miss about this relationship is _____.

When I think about staying, I feel _____.

CHOOSING TO STAY

> "Trying to change him was like rolling a large stone up a mountain, only to have it fall down and crush you. Now I just focus on myself."
>
> HELEN

Every day that you remain in a relationship, you are making a decision to stay. Whether you make that choice intentionally or not is up to you. But when the choice is conscious, you derive the benefit of knowing that you are in control of one very important aspect of your own life, not out of control.

Of course, it can be difficult to know whether to stay in a relationship or to leave it. If you are recovering from addictive love, your decision is more complex. But as you change, giving more love to yourself, you become less dependent and less addicted, and the dynamics of the relationship are given a chance to change for the better.

If the dynamics of your relationship do not change, you will have discovered some valuable information about yourself, your partner, and the prognosis for the future. You will then be in a better and stronger position to exercise your power of choice and to make your next decision.

If you are uncertain about whether to stay in your present relationship, answering these questions can help you to clarify your thoughts and feelings.

In this relationship, I feel that my interests, opinions, and values

are (respected, not respected) _____.

When I think about staying, the feelings that come up most are

(happiness, resentment, relief, anger) _____.

When I listen to my inner voice concerning this relationship, it

tells me _____.

What I liked most about this relationship in the first place was

_____.

What upsets me about this relationship is _____.

Of pleasure or pain, the aspect that is greater in this relation-

ship is _____.

The compelling reason for making the decision I am making is

_____.

DECIDING TO LOVE

> " To love somebody is not just a strong feeling—it is a decision, it is a judgment, it is a promise. "
>
> ERICH FROMM

If you are not currently in a relationship, or if your current relationship ever ends, you will at some point face the choice of whether or not to become involved with someone else. Deciding to love is a decision you alone can make, and a very important one. It determines whether you will continue the cycle of addiction to destructive relationships or break free from it at last.

The following exercise can help you to decide whether to begin an intimate relationship with a prospective partner, and whether to deepen it later if you do.

When I am with _____, I feel as if I am (intelligent, stupid, talented, clumsy, gorgeous, overweight, lively, old, worthy, unworthy, etc.) _____.

When I listen to this man, I generally (like, dislike) _____ what he has to say.

After I spend several hours with _____, I feel (drained or replenished) _____.

This man appears to be (for example, loving, unloving, generous, strong, withdrawn, giving, demanding) _____.

With this man, I can be (my whole self, a partial self) _____

_____.

What we have in common is _____.

What we don't have in common is _____.

By observing this man's words and actions, I would conclude that he is (capable of intimacy, incapable of intimacy) _____

_____.

In this relationship, I (will, will not) _____ be able to grow.

My feelings for this man are generally (for example, loving, confused, excited, fearful) _____.

CHOOSING TO MAKE LOVE

> "I finally decided that sex is optional—not like one of the compulsory moves in a gymnastics meet."
>
> CHRIS

One of the first critical steps in intimate relationships is deciding whether and when to make love. Many women in addictive-love relationships feel that they have little choice in this matter, and that if they do not make love on demand—when, where, and in a way that the other person wants—they will lose him. This is true only when a man is unusually focused on himself. In that case, he is a poor choice for real intimacy anyway.

When deciding whether it makes sense to become sexually involved with someone, ask yourself the following questions:

When I touch this man, my gestures of affection feel (authentic, inauthentic) _____.

When he touches me, I feel (cared for, invaded, appreciated, overpowered) _____.

If I were to make love to this man, I think that afterward I would feel (angry, resentful, loved, satisfied, content) _____.

To me, sex means _____.

To him, I think that sex means _____.

Whether or not I am involved in a romantic, sexual relationship with this man, I (can, cannot) _____ feel like a sexual being.

I feel pressure coming from (him, myself, no one) _____ to perform sexually.

The most intense feeling I have for this man is one of (for example, caring, rapport, respect, fear, animal magnetism) _____.

Someone to whom I feel physically attracted but do not like is _____.

Someone for whom I do not feel a strong physical attraction but whom I have tender feelings for is _____.

Your answers to all of the above questions may help you to clarify your feelings and to decide whether choosing to make love at this time would be more beneficial or detrimental. The last two questions are especially helpful for putting physical attraction in perspective.

CHANGING THE THINGS YOU CAN

"God, grant me the serenity to accept the things I cannot change, the courage to change the things I can, and the wisdom to know the difference."

SERENITY PRAYER

Recovery is taking place when you know instinctively when to take the power and make a choice, and when to let go.

In this section you will begin to see the following three things clearly:

1. You have the power to make choices concerning your own life.

2. You have no power to control the actions of others.

3. Sometimes you share power with others.

Now, take a piece of paper and divide it into three vertical columns. Head them according to the chart below. Under the appropriate column, write down the areas in your life over which you feel you have no power, feel you share power, and feel you have real power.

Powerless (No Responsibility)	Shared Power (Shared Responsibility)	Power (Responsibility)

One woman's list looked like this:

Powerless (No Responsibility)	Shared Power (Shared Responsibility)	Power (Responsibility)
International politics	Human relationships	My actions
Weather		My attitudes
Other people's actions		Decisions affecting my life
Other people's opinions of me		
Results		My priorities
My emotions		How I act on my emotions

In your life, are there any areas for which you no longer have to take complete responsibility? Write them here.

_____

_____

How does this feel to you?

_____

_____

Do you recognize any power you never knew you had?

_____

_____

Now look at the items on your list under the left-hand column. You are powerless over these areas. You have as little control over your boyfriend's actions as you have over hurricanes in Florida or warfare in the Persian Gulf.

You share the power to make decisions in the area of human relationships, but you are powerless over results. So it is wise not to worry too much over outcomes in these two areas.

Now look at the right-hand column. You have power over—and can take full responsibility for—the items listed here. You are the sole owner of your actions, attitudes, and priorities. You do not have power over your emotions, but you do have power over how you choose to act on them.

CHOOSING WHAT IS BEST FOR YOU

> **"I am starting to trust my own instincts."**
>
> STEPHANIE

You will know that you are taking control of your power to choose when (check any breakthroughs you have already made):

_____ You almost give away your power to choose, but then you remember that you do have this power and make a start at claiming it.

_____ You know and respect your own conditions for entering a relationship.

_____ You gracefully get out of a relationship that was or would have been destructive to you.

_____ You are willing to experiment by talking to people who may not be "your type."

_____ You are willing to experience the temporary discomfort of healthy choice, knowing that these feelings will diminish as you continue to make the choices that are best for you.

_____ If someone cannot understand your point of view, you no longer take this as a signal to try harder. You can let go.

_____ When the opportunity for a glamorous but addictive relationship comes your way, you're not interested.

_____ When the possibility of a healthy relationship comes your way, you give it a chance, whether or not anything comes of it.

_____ You make a choice you could not have made six months, or six weeks, ago.

_____ You appreciate how far you have come in your recovery.

The Turning Point: Paulette

Paulette, twenty-nine, is an emergency-room nurse living in Portland, Oregon. She is slim, with very dark hair and a creamy complexion. In a clear voice, she speaks slowly at first, and then rushes in sudden bursts of enthusiasm.

Paulette was raised in a typical upper-middle-class dysfunctional family. Her mother, a housewife, was an alcoholic, while her father was absent, preoccupied with work. Like many children from dysfunctional families, Paulette took to heart a message she received at home: "Don't feel."

This alienation from her feelings adversely affected her adult relationships—until she joined a peer group, found a supportive therapist, and started to change. Here, she tells how reawakened feelings helped her to make a difficult decision.

Bob and I have lived together for eight years. After the second year, I wanted to leave, but I felt a strong pull to stay. While Bob often acted coldly toward me, the more I was rejected, the harder I tried to make him care. I felt that because my struggle was great, my reward would be that much greater when he stopped rejecting me. I'm sure this was a continuation of my futile efforts to earn my parents' love. If I could change Bob's rejection to acceptance, that would be the biggest triumph.

One way he rejected me was in bed. After the second year, Bob told me he was not interested in sex with me. On the street, he would point out well-endowed women, whom he was sexually interested in. I would try to seduce him and would usually be rejected. The only feelings I knew were the excitement and challenge of trying to win him over.

After a year in support groups and therapy, I had developed more self-esteem. I was feeling confident enough to stop fighting my feelings. I started to give my feelings respect.

I have a wristwatch that chimes every hour. Every time it chimed, I would ask myself, "How am I feeling right now?" When I checked in with myself several times a day, I noticed how often I felt angry with Bob or stressed out from the strain of trying to make our relationship work. The constant sexual rejection was the hardest feeling to pay attention to.

This is not to say that my feelings were totally negative. There were good things about our relationship. We had fun; we had good talks. I wish Bob weren't so damn cute. I still feel strongly physically attracted to him. But the painful feelings far outweighed the positive ones.

For many years I was afraid of my feelings, because I thought I would be swallowed up by them. I had always felt like a helpless child. But in my therapist's office, I had a reunion with the adult in me that I never knew existed. After I had a conversation between my inner parent and child, I recognized that my inner parent was very strong. I knew that I could always count on myself. I felt a strong sense of hope about the future—a feeling that I'd never had before.

When my self-esteem was low, I had thought that the pain of separating from Bob would be insurmountable. I did not think I had the strength to survive a breakup. But after that turning point when I felt I had a strong inner adult, I knew I deserved more than constant rejection. Now I felt a sense of hope that there was a better relationship possible for me. I decided to leave.

Once I had made the decision, the fear of abandonment came up, and that was very scary. One day I was riding my bike through the woods, and I was overcome by a wave of pain and sadness at the thought of separating. Instead of fighting the sadness, I let the feelings wash over me and through me. At that moment, I thought, "If this is as bad as the pain is going to get, I can stand it." The only way I can combat the pain is to give a lot of love to myself.

I have friends in my groups who support me. I have my therapist. I treat myself as a mother would treat a daughter she cared a lot about. Sometimes I say affirmations into a cassette recorder and play the message back.

A new sense of spirituality is helping me to get through this separation. I know that there is someone I've been growing into—and that this relationship has been impeding that growth. If I'm connected to the spiritual, that's fulfilling. I don't necessarily have to be connected to a man.

When I told Bob I wanted to leave, he didn't protest. He rarely asks for what he wants. In the past, I would have been paralyzed with worry over what would happen to Bob without me. Now I know that he has to find his own way. It's not helping him for me to stay.

While I rely on my feelings, I also think things through. When the pain feels terrible and I think, "I'm going to die without Bob," I examine that belief to get to the truth. I ask myself, "What does this pain remind me of?" and I realize that it reminds me of my early emotional abandonment. I know that as an adult, I don't need Bob in the same way I needed my parents when I was a child. I can rely on myself, as well as on my friends.

I feel renewed and positive. I have been saving money for years, and I've bought myself a house. I'm learning to take care of myself—financially, spiritually, and emotionally.

CHAPTER 10

Increasing Your Capacity
for Healthy Intimacy

> " Genuine love is precious and is best spent on those who will accept it and return it. "
>
> SHARON WEGSCHEIDER-CRUSE

The final challenge of recovery is healthy intimacy. As we grow stronger ourselves, we find that we are more likely to choose a partner who is strong enough to return our love. While toxic relationships required us to do all the giving, healthy, "smart" love gives back to us. Smart love reassures us by its constancy and caring. It enhances our lives and our sense of self.

Despite the advantages of enjoying healthy relationships, many of us fear intimacy. In this last stage of recovery, we must be willing to look at our own fears about intimacy, and at whether these have led us to choose impossible relationships, to sabotage healthy relationships, to send mixed messages, or to stay out of close relationships altogether for fear of letting ourselves be known.

Each reader will define intimacy for herself. One definition of intimacy is allowing another person to see us exactly as we are—by talking about who we really are and what we are feeling, saying what we want and need, and being heard by an intimate partner. This may involve being able to tell a close friend or mate how humbled and defeated we are feeling at a particular moment, rather than pretending to be cheerful and confident all the time. It may mean making our needs explicit rather than keeping quiet about them.

Healthy intimacy also involves accepting inevitable differences. It may mean asking your intimate partner what a particular experience was like for him, rather than assuming that his experience was identical to yours.

To be honest, vulnerable, and accepting of differences contradicts the survival skills many of us acquired growing up in dysfunctional families. In childhood, many of us learned that we could receive love and approval only by acting exactly the way our parents wanted us to. As a result, as adults we may have felt that we could receive love and approval only by trying to be what we thought other people—especially the men in our lives—wanted us to be. But in fact, a healthy friend or mate will encourage us to be ourselves, even when we disagree with that person about something.

Fortunately, we can release ourselves from past programming. With information and practice, we can learn the skills that enhance healthy intimacy.

Recovery from addictive love does not require you to develop a romantic relationship. While, in its healthiest form, this is certainly a wonderful and desirable situation, it is not needed for recovery. But developing your capacity for intimacy with others remains an important part of recovery. Every exercise in this chapter may be practiced with either a romantic partner or a friend.

It was our thinking of romantic relationships as being very different from close friendships that led us into destructive romantic patterns in the first place. As our recovery continues, we will realize that healthy romantic relationships emerge from deep, trusting friendships.

Does all the talk about friendship mean the end of good sex? Not at all. As author Janet Geringer-Woititz says, "In a healthy relationship, you still have chemistry, but the energy doesn't come from abusing each other."

One of the surprising results of the interviews I conducted for this book concerned sexual satisfaction among women in healthy relationships. Only two of the women I interviewed said that they had felt a "charge" when they first met their partners. Many more women reported that their relationships had developed slowly. And while sex with a man they had gotten to know gradually, as a companion, had been somewhat disappointing at first, in time it became the most satisfying sex they had known. The feelings grew as they came to learn each other both emotionally and sexually.

True intimacy is "being known": revealing and sharing your real self with another person as he reveals and shares himself with you. This is not easy. It takes courage to reveal oneself to another human being. The source of this courage is autonomy. We develop the strength to say what is true for us and to choose what is best for us. Then, if we enter into a relationship, we are still independent and self-determining. It is this autonomy, this ability to look after ourselves, that enables us to feel free of worries about being abandoned. And when we are autonomous, the man in our life will not feel smothered.

In healthy intimate relationships, we are strong enough to express our feelings and opinions and caring enough to value the feelings and opinions of someone else. In smart, healthy love, we balance our awareness of pleasing others with a growing awareness of what pleases *us*. You have probably already experienced healthy intimacy. Since you started reading this book, you may have revealed your honest feelings to yourself, to close friends, or to new friends in support groups.

Whether or not you are currently in a romantic relationship, as you recover from addictive love you will find that your capacity for healthy intimacy will increase.

RECOGNIZING HEALTHY INTIMACY

Are your intimate relationships healthy or toxic? How can you tell one from the other? Of course, no relationship is totally healthy or totally addictive. But the following chart can help you to evaluate the general nature of your relationships.

TOXIC INTIMACY	HEALTHY INTIMACY
Obsession with finding "someone to love"	Development of self as a first priority
Need for immediate gratification	Desire for long-term contentment; relationship develops step by step
Pressuring partner for sex or commitment	Freedom of choice
Imbalance of power	Balance and mutuality in the relationship
Power plays for control	Compromise, negotiation or taking turns at leading
No-talk rule, especially if things are not working out	Sharing wants, feelings, and appreciation of what your partner means to you
Manipulation	Directness
Lack of trust	Appropriate trust (that is, knowing that your partner will likely behave according to his fundamental nature)
Attempts to change partner to meet one's needs	Embracing of each other's individuality
Relationship is based on delusion and avoidance of the unpleasant	Relationship deals with all aspects of reality
Relationship is always the same	Relationship is always changing
Expectation that one partner will fix and rescue the other	Self-care by both partners
Fusion (being obsessed with each other's problems and feelings)	Loving detachment (healthy concern about partner's well-being and growth, while letting go)
Passion confused with fear	Sex grows out of friendship and caring
Blaming self or partner for problems	Problem-solving together
Cycle of pain and despair	Cycle of comfort and contentment

This list was compiled after listening to a lecture on intimacy by Chicago therapist Terence Gorski.

PRETENDING

If we were taught to be inauthentic as children, we learned to pretend that our feelings or values were different from what they are. Such pretending blocks healthy intimacy. We tend to think that if we take down our masks, the other person will leave us. But in a healthy relationship, the other person sees who we are—and loves us anyway.

Some common pretenses adopted by those in addictive relationships include lying to partners about their interests ("Sure, I'd love to try snow camping!"), lying about their goals ("Me, too! I never want to live with anyone again"), or lying about their values ("I'm a very spiritual person").

Sharing the truth creates intimacy. Even difficult truths can bring you closer together.

This exercise will help you to identify areas in which you are currently being inauthentic.

I pretend that (check those that apply):

_____ I have more education than I have.

_____ I have a better job than I do.

_____ I come from a wealthier family.

_____ I am cheerful and "up" all the time.

_____ I am energetic all the time.

_____ I know more than I do sexually.

_____ I am sexually aroused when I am not.

_____ I am orgasmic when I am not.

_____ I am always strong.

_____ I never need help.

_____ I have perfect relationships with others (when I actually have a very typical mix of problems and compatibility).

_____ My romantic relationship is wonderful, even when I feel that it is especially shaky.

Now that you have begun to see some of the areas in which you have been pretending, you can learn how to break free of this pattern and create a climate in which healthy intimacy can flourish.

SAYING WHAT YOU WANT

> **"**I shall become a master in this art only after a great deal of practice.**"**
>
> ERICH FROMM

In order to achieve true intimacy, we need to take the risk of saying exactly what we think, how we feel, and what we want. When we stop trying to please others by pretending that we always echo their opinions or experiences, we develop a more solid sense of who we are, as well as a respect for individual difference and diversity.

Many women first experience healthy intimacy in Twelve-Step program meetings and after meetings at coffee, where the honest level of sharing continues. These women find that they can then transfer the skills they have learned to all of their intimate relationships.

Remember, there is no true intimacy between two partners until they can both express their wants. When either or both are forced to deny essential parts of themselves, they are acting out a pretense. A pretense is not intimacy.

You can begin to increase your capacity for intimacy by telling another person—a close friend, a member of your group, or your partner—about your feelings, thoughts, and motives, and by listening to his or hers. Ask this person to practice the following exercise with you.

Sit down with your friend or partner, and take turns doing this exercise. The person who begins says the following to the other out loud, filling in the blanks as honestly as he or she can. Then the other person does the same.

Practice this exercise once or twice a week for several

weeks, or every night for one week. At each session, do the complete exercise four or five times.

I want _____.

I need _____.

I feel _____.

I'm afraid _____.

The way I see it, _____.

I prefer _____ to _____.

I'm so glad that _____.

KNOWING WHEN TO KEEP QUIET

You can also increase your capacity for healthy intimacy by learning when to be quiet. Some things are better left unsaid.

Some of the times when *not* talking or expressing feelings is in the best interests of the relationship might be:

- When your partner is talking.

- When what you feel like saying would be destructive to the relationship ("You're just like your father" or "You've always had terrible taste"). Notice that these are typically "you" statements.

- When there is any feeling of "Gotcha!" to what you are about to say.

- When you think of something especially clever and sarcastic.

- When what you are about to say would be a great and unnecessary burden to your partner (for example, telling a new lover the number of lovers you have had in the past).

- When you are about to attempt to manipulate, pressure, or control your partner.

- When your sentence starts with "To be perfectly frank . . ."

UNDERSTANDING YOUR PARTNER

The preceding exercises helped you to learn to express your thoughts and feelings to your partner and to solicit and listen to his. You can increase your capacity for intimacy by understanding your partner's feelings. Many codependents are very giving, yet do not always understand where the other person is "coming from." We try to read the mind of a close friend or partner, assuming we know what he's thinking or feeling. Assumptions are often wrong; sometimes we need to ask.

So that you do not try to read your partner's mind, practice asking the following questions aloud.

"Do you want my help—or would you rather be left alone?"

"Are you disappointed—or relieved?"

"Is this important to you?"

"Is this hard for you?"

"Do you want to talk about it?"

Asking questions such as these will lead you to understand what a certain experience is like for your partner. This deep level of understanding is called empathy, a key component of any successful friendship.

When you learn to say what you want and to ask questions that lead to empathy, the nature of your relationship will deepen, and stronger bonds of intimacy will be forged.

EMPATHY WITHOUT OVERINVOLVEMENT

"In contrast to symbiotic union, love is union under the condition of preserving one's integrity, one's individuality."

ERICH FROMM

The next exercise will help you to understand your partner's point of view or feelings, while maintaining your own. In an empathic response, you are emotionally connected to the other person, but you are still aware that his feelings are his own.

It is a hallmark of a dysfunctional relationship to actually feel a partner's pain or to take on his problems. As noted in chapter 7 ("Defining Your Boundaries"), therapists sometimes refer to this as "projective identification." In this dysfunctional response, we experience the feelings of another as if they were our own. For example, if our partner is having feelings of low self-esteem, we begin to feel insecure about ourselves. We may have learned in childhood that "Mommy and I are one" (as though no boundaries existed), and so we naturally take on the problems and pain of those around us.

If you are having a problem in experiencing the separateness of your partner's feelings, first become very clear on how *you* feel.

I am feeling _____ right now.

The way I see it, _____

_____

_____.

Next, turn to your partner and ask an appropriate question ("Is this how you see it?" or "Is this how you're feeling?") Or guess—and acknowledge the guess ("I'm guessing—is this how you see it?").

Do not take on his feelings. Simply see his point of view and

restate it: "It seems to me that what you're feeling right now is

_____.

After you have repeated to your partner what he has just told you, complete the following sentences:

If I saw the situation through _____'s

eyes, it might look like _____.

If I had _____'s fundamental nature, I might be feeling _____ right now.

If I were _____, the truth for me right now might be _____.

Now come back to yourself.

My point of view on this matter is _____.

My feelings right now are _____.

The truth for me right now is _____.

Now let your partner know your point of view, your feelings, and the truth you perceive. Hold on to your own truth, but look at how your partner's truth might be different—and why. At first, this process may seem very slow, but in time healthy empathy will become easier and more automatic.

INTIMATE CONNECTIONS

> " Love does not consist of gazing at each other but in looking outward in the same direction. "
>
> ANTOINE DE SAINT-EXUPÉRY

Healthy intimacy is more difficult to achieve when the values, goals, or activities you wish to share are outside of your partner's sphere of interest. We are more likely to have healthy intimacy when we share much of ourselves with our partners, when we make emotional connections in areas that are important to us. You can increase your chances for healthy intimacy by choosing a partner whose interests, values, and goals connect with yours in several key areas.

Obviously, connections in some areas are more important than in others. For example, sharing musical tastes is less important than sharing basic values. If one person thinks it is all right to have sex with a different partner but the other does not, the bond probably will not last. If one considers making money to be a very high priority but the other does not, a strain in the relationship will result. Likewise, if you do not share goals there is little chance the relationship will be healthy. The following exercises will help you to check your compatibility of values, interests, and goals with a potential partner.

Shared Values

As you get to know a potential partner, you will naturally discover your shared values about life. But if you want to speed up the process of getting acquainted in order to evaluate compatibility, you can ask the other person about his personal values in these areas of life. After doing so, check those you know to be compatible:

Spiritual and intellectual values

_____ Spirituality

_____ Philosophy

_____ Intellectuality

_____ Values

_____ Goals

Social and emotional values

_____ Emotional expression

_____ Social life

_____ Parenting (mutual nurturing)

Physical and practical areas

_____ Sexuality

_____ Finances

Shared Interests

While the sharing of values and interests are interconnected, it can be useful to evaluate interests separately. You do not, of course, need to share all of your interests with your partner.

Some can be shared with other friends or family members; others can be done alone. However, you and your partner should be able to do together a good percentage of the activities that you both enjoy. And you should be able to discuss openly how you are thinking and feeling about those that you do not do together. In this way, you can grow from each other's experiences. And remember (from the chapter on boundaries) that you do not have to match opinions. For example, you can argue about politics and still have a good political connection as long as you're both interested in the subject.

Following are some activities that women interviewed for this book reported sharing with their partners; place a check mark next to those that apply to you and your partner.

Spiritual and intellectual interests

_____   Meditation

_____   Philosophical talks

_____   Discussing and reading about spirituality

_____   Visiting museums

_____   Attending concerts

_____   Going to church or synagogue

_____   Politics and world affairs

_____   Exploring nature

Social and emotional interests

_____   Friends in common

_____   Parenting

_____   Dancing

_____   Conversation

_____   Going to movies

_____   Cooking

_____   Parties and other social events

_____   Humor

Physical and practical interests

_____ Sex

_____ Affection

_____ Running

_____ Hiking

_____ Bike riding

_____ Skiing

_____ Tennis

_____ Travel

_____ Scuba diving

_____ Financial planning

CHOOSING AN APPROPRIATE PARTNER

Clearly, healthy intimacy is not one-sided. It requires two healthy people. You cannot, therefore, have a healthy relationship with someone who is incapable of intimacy.

If you were taught to avoid intimacy as a child, you may have continued to avoid it as an adult by choosing dangerous, inappropriate, or unavailable partners. You can break free of this pattern by learning how to choose partners with whom real intimacy is possible, and by learning how to avoid men who are inappropriate partners. You can begin to do this by asking potential partners about their preferences, goals, and feelings, and by listening carefully to their answers.

You also need to know your own conditions for entering a relationship, and you need to learn to move slowly into intimacy.

The following checklist is designed to help you determine a partner's capacity for intimacy. Answer "T" for True and "F" for False.

1. _____ He occasionally says, "I blew it." He can admit he has made a mistake.

2. _____ When you have a success, he feels free to say, "I'm really happy you got that raise—and I'm also envious."

3. _____ You explain and explain, but he can never quite understand your point of view.

4. _____ He basks in the warm glow of your praise. You, however, are allowed very few compliments.

5. _____ He says, "I don't have to tell you I love you. After all, I'm here, aren't I?"

6. _____ He says he likes women far too much to limit himself to one lover.

7. _____ He introduces you to his friends, and he wants to meet your parents.

8. _____ He has a pattern of promising to arrive or call and then not following through—but his excuses are golden.

9. _____ He says that "someone has to be the boss, and it is up to the man to lead."

10. _____ He says, "I'm really angry with you."

11. _____ He implies that you two could have a good thing going if only you weren't so flawed.

12. _____ He lets you know through his words and actions that he is awfully glad you're in his life.

13. _____ He listens.

"True" answers to statements 1, 2, 7, 10, 12, or 13 are positive signs. Statement 1 demonstrates your partner's ability to be honest and admit imperfection. Statements 2 and 10 show that he is capable of expressing even so-called "negative" feelings; this is very healthy, because he has learned to be honest about his emotions and does not hide them. Statement 7 indicates that he is able to think seriously about commitment, while 12 and 13 indicate that he is capable of both showing affection and relating to you on a deeper level.

"True" answers to statements 3, 4, 5, 6, 8, 9, or 11 are unhealthy signs. Statement 3 indicates that he cannot share or understand—both prerequisites to intimacy. Statements 4 and 5 show that he is unwilling or unable to express appreciation for you—and no one can be intimate with someone he or she does not appreciate. Statement 6 shows that he is not currently interested in or capable of commitment. Statement 8 shows that he is acting irresponsibly, which precludes healthy intimacy. Statement 9 shows that he believes he has the right to dominate his partner and ignore her needs and wishes, while 11 demonstrates that he focuses more on a partner's minuses than on pluses.

SAFE INTIMACY

> " There is the risk you cannot afford to take, (and) there is the risk you cannot afford *not* to take. "
>
> PETER DRUCKER (MANAGEMENT EXPERT/AUTHOR)

These days, love and intimacy require us to take certain risks. In addition to the danger of contracting AIDS, there is the possibility of ending up with a dangerous, abusive, or self-destructive partner. But there are "unsafe" and "safe" risks. Unsafe-risk, or high-risk, situations include becoming involved with a dominant partner or an active alcoholic, or having sex on the first date. Every woman in this book who is now in a good relationship took a safe risk in entering that relationship.

This exercise will help you to determine which risks are safe for you and which feel too dangerous.

1. For me, "complete safety" involves (for example, refusing to answer the phone, refusing all invitations)

   _____

   _____

   _____

2. A risk I am not willing to take would be (giving my phone number to a stranger, having sex on the first date, having sex with someone who uses I.V. drugs, having unsafe sex, becoming involved with a married man or an active alcoholic)

    _____

    _____

    _____

    _____

3. A risk I am willing to take would be (going to a party, talking to strangers at a party, talking to a stranger in a bookstore, asking someone for his or her phone number, calling an old friend, being friendlier to other people, accepting a date with someone who is "not my type")

    _____

    _____

    _____

PRACTICING HEALTHY INTIMACY

Place a check mark by any of the following steps you have already taken toward practicing healthy intimacy.

_____ Your friendships and relationships are balanced. No one has all the power, and no one does all the giving.

_____ You respect each other's freedom of choice. Neither person pressures the other to deepen the relationship or to become sexual before the other is ready.

_____ You can let your friends be exactly who they are, even if you don't like everything about them. You do not need to change them to meet your needs.

_____ You check a situation for safety and trust before you reveal an intimate detail of your life.

_____ Even when you enter a romantic relationship, you continue to see your other friends, and you continue your own nurturing rituals.

The Turning Point: Dominique

Dominique, thirty-eight, is a brunette whose most arresting feature is her blue eyes. She gestures expressively, using her hands when telling a dramatic story. She works as a children's book editor; she lives in suburban Connecticut and commutes to New York City.

Before Dominique's recovery, all of her relationships with men had been distant. Her father, a brilliant mathematician and an alcoholic, ignored his wife's ploys to attract his attention to Dominique by dressing her in a new dress. "That's nice," he would say, returning to his gin and his work.

Like her father, Dominique learned that she could numb painful feelings and mask shyness with alcohol. Her first husband, Ryan, a writer, was movie-star handsome, witty, and aloof. The couple had separate bedrooms, and their nightly drinking only increased the distance between them. Ryan would retire to his room, lock the door, and drink and write. Dominique would pound on his door, pleading, "Please pay some attention to me," repeating the painful drama of her childhood.

Dominique's second husband, Alan, a musician, was also handsome, charismatic, and unattainable. This time, distance in the relationship was maintained through her drinking, his use of cocaine, and the presence of Alan's fans in the house at all hours. Three months into the marriage, Alan became physically abusive. When the violence escalated, Dominique left, sought the help of a therapist, and joined a group for battered women.

Her therapist helped her to notice the times when she used alcohol to avoid painful feelings about her two failed marriages. No longer could Dominique remain distant from herself. Now she knew precisely what she was feeling. She learned that if she courageously rode out a feeling, it would always pass. Her drinking diminished, then stopped.

With her therapist, Dominique explored her needs and wants in a relationship. While in the past she had always chosen distant men, in becoming more intimate with herself she realized that she wanted a different kind of relationship. But when she finally met an open, genuinely intimate man who wanted to be close, Dominique had to overcome her own fears about intimacy.

Two months after I stopped drinking, I went to a party. In a corner was this dark, handsome, brooding, aloof guy. I felt this strong magnetic attraction. I had to literally p-u-u-u-l-l-l myself away from him. By then I had learned that he was exactly the man I should avoid.

At this same party, I met Mike. He was a friendly, pleasant-looking man, but I didn't feel any magnetic pull. Mike asked me to leave the party and go to a bar with him. I said, "No, I'm enjoying myself, but here's my card if you'd like to call me." Because I had learned early in life to please men and go along with what they wanted to do, I was proud of myself for standing up to him.

A month later, on a Saturday night, Mike called. "I'm kind of a spontaneous guy," he said, "and I was wondering if you'd like to get together tonight." I told him I was busy that night and that I generally planned my life ahead. Again, I was letting him know what I liked and didn't like. There was a two-second pause. Then he said, "How about next Saturday night?"

Before the date, I told myself I didn't have to be cute or funny. I was dropping the roles I had played with men. There was an absolute insistence that I was going to be myself.

Mike and I went to a restaurant and did not drink, so I could not rely on alcohol to smooth away my shyness or bring out my party-girl persona. It was uncomfortable having to really be me and letting him accept me or reject me.

The very next day, he called to tell me what a good time he had had and to ask me out for the next weekend. From then on, he always called me the day after our date. I could see the consistency: he was going to keep acting the same way. I started to trust him.

There are layers of intimacy. I was frightened that Mike might not like me on the sixth layer. A month after we began dating, we started making love, and I felt even more exposed than ever. There was a palpable uncomfortableness, a nervous feeling in my chest and stomach. I felt extremely vulnerable. We talked about it. I said, "I like you so much. Why do I feel so uncomfortable with you?" I finally figured it out: this must be a fear of intimacy.

This was not the same kind of nervousness I had felt with men who were judgmental or who pulled away from me. They never really saw me, so I did not have to fear being exposed.

Mike was open about who he was, who he had been, who he wanted to be, and how he felt about me. Mike looked right through me. He wanted to know who I was, and he wouldn't tolerate any games. There was no hiding. I was accustomed to the safety of distant relationships.

The turning point in our relationship came when we were both terrified of what might happen. We had both been burned a lot in relationships, and we talked about how we were feeling. He was as scared as I was.

Alcoholics are cowards. I had always numbed uncomfortable feelings with alcohol. I couldn't do that anymore. Mike had already learned the lesson about having to go through whatever feelings he had. He knew that feelings always pass. We decided to just be with each other and see what happened. It was uncomfortable having him admire me and like me. It was uncomfortable having him love me. But I stayed with the feelings and experienced them, no matter how uncomfortable they were at the time.

Within six months, those scared, nervous feelings we both felt had dwindled. And by the time we had moved in together, they had disappeared.

Six months later, we were married. Intimacy grows deeper. You let your guard down more as time goes by. We've only known each other for three years. I wish it were twenty. I feel like this bath of warm honey is being poured on me because Mike is so loving. This had never been the norm for me.

How to Start Your Own Support Group*

First, learn what resources are already available in the area you live in. Often, communities have a directory listing all service agencies and sources of help. If you don't know whether such a publication exists or how to find it, call your library or your community crisis hotline. (Also, see Appendix II for a listing of groups nationwide. You can call or write to them, and they will advise you regarding local service agencies.) In addition, most telephone directories now include a "Human Services" listing, so you can check that as well.

Do not, however, assume that one phone call to one agency or professional will result in all the information you need to have. It is difficult for any professional in a large community to stay in touch with all the resources that the area has to offer, and, unfortunately, many professionals are woefully uninformed about what is currently available.

Do your own homework. Make the calls you need, anonymously if you wish. See if the group you need already exists. There's no point reinventing the wheel or going into competition with a group that is already functioning and could use your involvement. If you are a candidate for Daughters United, Overeaters Anonymous, Al-Anon, Shelter Services groups for

*Reprinted from *Women Who Love Too Much* by Robin Norwood (Jeremy P. Tarcher, Inc.)

163

battered women, or Crisis groups for rape survivors, be willing
to take some time and go to some trouble—maybe traveling
some distance—to attend the meetings they offer. It will be
worth it to you.

If, after diligent searching, you are quite certain that the
group you need doesn't exist, start one yourself.

Probably the best way to begin is to run an ad in the person-
als section of your newspaper. It might go something like this:

> WOMEN: Has falling in love meant being in emotional pain
> sooner or later? A free self-help group is now forming for
> women whose relationships with men have, up to now, usu-
> ally been destructive. If you want to overcome this problem,
> call [your first name and phone number] for information and
> location of meeting.

You should be able to fill a group by running such an ad just
a few times. Ideally, your group would have about seven to
twelve members, but start with fewer if necessary.

Remember, at that first meeting the women who show up
are there because this is a serious problem for them and they
are looking for help. Don't spend too much of the meeting time
talking about how to organize future meetings, even though
that, too, is important. The best way to start is to share your
stories, because doing so will forge an immediate bond and a
sense of belonging. Women who love too much are much more
alike than different, and that will be felt by all of you. So make
sharing your stories your first priority.

Try this agenda for your first meeting, which should last no
more than an hour:

1. Start on time. This lets everyone involved know that they
must be prompt for future meetings.

2. Introduce yourself as the person who ran the ad, and explain
that you would like the group to develop into a continuing
source of support for yourself and everyone present.

3. Emphasize that everything that is said during the meeting
is to remain in the meeting, that no one who is seen there or

anything that is said there should be discussed elsewhere, *ever.* Suggest that those present simply use their first names to introduce themselves.

4. Explain that it would probably help everyone there to hear one another's reasons for coming to the group and that perhaps each person could talk for up to five minutes about what made her decide to come. Emphasize that no one has to talk for that long, but that this amount of time is available to each person should she want it. Volunteer to begin by giving your first name and telling your own story briefly.

5. When everyone who wants to do so has shared her story, go back to those who did not want to talk when it was their turn, and gently ask if they would like to now. Do not pressure anyone to speak. Make it very clear that each woman is welcome whether or not she is ready to talk about her situation yet.

6. Now talk about some of the guidelines that you would like to see the group follow. I recommend the following, which should be copied down and given to each participant:

No advice giving.   All are welcome to share their experiences and what has worked to help them feel better, but no one should advise another as to what she should do. Advice giving should be gently pointed out if anyone indulges in it.

Leadership should rotate within the group weekly, so that each meeting is led by a different member.   It is the leader's responsibility to start the meeting on time, to pick a topic to be discussed, to save a few minutes at the end for any business matters, and to choose another leader for the following week before she closes the meeting.

Meetings should last a specific length of time.   I recommend one hour. No one is going to solve all her problems in one meeting, and it is important not to try to do so. Meetings should start promptly and end on time. (It is better that they be too short than too long. Members can decide to lengthen the meeting if they wish, later on.)

The meeting place should be a neutral setting rather than someone's home, if at all possible.   Homes are full of distractions: children, telephone calls, and lack of privacy for the group members, especially the hostess. Moreover, the role of hostess should be avoided. You are not entertaining one another socially; you are working together as peers to recover from your common problems. Many banks, businesses, and churches make rooms available free of charge to groups for meetings in the evening hours.

No eating, drinking of beverages, or smoking while the meeting is in progress.   These all serve to distract from the business at hand. Such things may be made available before and after the meeting if your group decides that this is important. *Never* provide alcohol. It distorts people's feelings and reactions and impedes the work to be done.

Avoid talking about "him."   This is *very* important. Group members must learn to focus on themselves and on their own thoughts, feelings, and behaviors rather than on the man who is their obsession. Some talking about him is inevitable at first, but as she shares each person should strive to keep this to the strictest minimum.

No one should be criticized about what she does or does not do, either when she is present or when she is absent from the group. Although members are free to ask for feedback from one another, this should never be given unsolicited. Like advice, criticism has no place in a support group.

Stick to the topic at hand.   Virtually any topic a leader wants to introduce is fine, with the exception of religion, politics, or outside issues (such as current events, celebrities, any causes, treatment programs, or therapeutic modalities). There is no room for debate or devisiveness in a support group. And remember, you are not meeting to gripe about men. You are interested in your own growth and healing, in sharing how you are developing new tools for coping with old problems. The following are some topic suggestions.

Why I need this group

Guilt and resentment

My worst fears

What I like best about myself and what I like least

How I take care of myself and meet my own needs

Loneliness

How I cope with depression

My sexual attitudes: what they are and where they come from

Anger: how I handle my own and others'

How I relate to men

What I think people think of me

Examining my motives

My responsibilities to myself; my responsibilities to others

My spirituality (this is *not* a discussion of religious beliefs, but of how each group member experiences her own spiritual dimension or doesn't)

Letting go of blame, including self-blame

Patterns in my life

It is recommended that group members read *Women Who Love Too Much,* but this is not a requirement, only a suggestion. You can also recommend using *Smart Love* together as a group.

The group may decide to add an extra fifteen minutes to the length of the meeting once a month to deal with business matters, format changes, how well the guidelines are working, or problems.

Now, back to the suggested format for the first meeting:

7. Discuss the list of guidelines together as a group.

8. Ask if someone would be willing to lead the group the following week.

9. Decide where the group will meet the following week and decide on the issue of refreshments before or after the meeting.

10. Discuss whether more women should be invited to join your group, whether to run the ad one more week, or whether the women present might invite other women.

11. Close the meeting by standing silently in a circle, holding hands, with eyes closed, for a few moments.

A final word regarding these guidelines: the principles of confidentiality, rotation of leadership, no criticism, no advice-giving, no discussions of controversial subjects or outside issues, no debating, and so on are all very important to group harmony and cohesion. Do not violate these principles in the interest of pleasing a group member. What is best for the group as a whole must always be considered first.

With this in mind, you have the basic tools for starting a group for women who love too much. Do not underestimate how very healing this simple hour's meeting of personal sharing will come to be in all of your lives. Together you are offering one another the opportunity to recover.

Relationship Addiction Recovery: Support Groups in the United States

This nationwide list of support groups can lead you to help in your area. However, new groups are forming all the time, and these groups are subject to change. So if you don't find what you need, please call your local women's center or YWCA for further information. Some states also have self-help information centers with toll-free hotlines.

ALABAMA

Huntsville

Kay B. Beasley, LCSW (205) 539-5717
Family Service Center
2003 Harvard Road
Huntsville, AL 35801

Dr. Lynne Abbott (205) 536-5511
The University of Alabama at Huntsville
109 Governor's Drive
Huntsville, AL 35801

ARIZONA

Phoenix

Contact numbers:
(602) 939-6798 / (602) 263-8856

Maryvale Samaritan Hospital
(602) 848-5000
5102 West Campbell
Phoenix, AZ 85035

Asbury Church (602) 279-2369
1601 Indian School Road
Phoenix, AZ 85015

Tempe

Carol Valentine, Ph.D. (602) 965-2358
Associate Director of Women's Studies
Arizona State University
Tempe, AZ 85287

Tri-City Community Behavioral Health
(602) 967-8685
1801 S. Jentilly #B8
Tempe, AZ 85281

ARKANSAS

Little Rock

Dr. Alda Moore (501) 661-1111

CALIFORNIA

Los Angeles County

Encino

Contact number: (818) 783-1707

Long Beach

Marion Solovei (213) 493-1496
Family Services of Long Beach
16704 Clark Avenue
Bellflower, CA 90705

Studio City

Dana Dovitch, Ph.D.
(818) 702-0170 / (818) 984-2626

Santa Monica and South Bay Area

Rhoda Pregerson (213) 391-2235

Arcadia

Santa Anita Counseling Center
(818) 574-3314
226 W. Colorado Place
Arcadia, CA 91005

Burbank

Nancy Golden (818) 509-5959
California Family Studies Center
5433 Laurel Canyon
No. Hollywood, CA 91607

Orange County

Contact number: (714) 831-1634

Riverside County

Moreno Valley

Rosanna Saputo (714) 924-8926

Palm Desert

Contact number: (619) 568-6551
73280 Highway 111, Suite 101
Palm Desert, CA 92260

San Diego County

Center for Women's Studies
    & Services
(619) 233-8984 / (619) 333-9141
(619) 233-3088

Association for Personal &
    Family Counseling
(619) 295-8595
7850 Mission Center Court, Suite 208
San Diego, CA 92108

ADC (619) 296-2419
P.O. Box 83037
San Diego, CA 92138-3037
Or:
2621 Denver Street, Suite A2
San Diego, CA 92110

Northern California

San Francisco

The Dry Dock Private Club
(415) 567-1775
2118 Greenwich (near Fillmore)
San Francisco, CA 94123

Fort Mason Center (415) 221-5058
Building C, Room 217
Buchanan Street & Marina Boulevard
San Francisco, CA 94123

Burlingame

Cheryl Gilbert (415) 696-5680
Peninsula Hospital
1848 El Camino Real
Burlingame, CA 94010

COLORADO

Denver Area

Womanschool Network (303) 238-7837
1005 Wadsworth Boulevard
Lakewood, CO 80215

Mary Jean Bedard (303) 922-9484
Serenity Counseling
6565 West Jewel #5
Lakewood, CO 80226

Linda Zika (303) 238-6399
1410 Vance Street #205
Lakewood, CO 80215

Sharon Wink (303) 797-5805
Arapahoe Community College
Resource Center—Women's Programs
5900 S. Santa Fe Drive
Littleton, CO 80160–9002

CONNECTICUT

Mystic

St. Mark's Episcopal Church
(203) 536-9521
Pearl Street
Mystic, CT 06355

WASHINGTON, DC AREA

Washington, DC

Christ Church Georgetown
(202) 333-6677
3116 'O' Street NW
Washington, DC 20007

Adelphi, MD

Women's Center & Referral Service
(301) 937-5265
Paint Branch Unitarian Church
3215 Powder Mill Road
Adelphi, MD 20783

Reston, VA

Carolyn (703) 435-3760
Washington Plaza Baptist Church
Lake Anne Plaza
Reston, VA 22090

Alexandria, VA

Lynnie (703) 255-3354
St. Paul's Episcopal Church,
  3rd Floor
Corner of Pitt & Duke Streets
Alexandria, VA 22314

DELAWARE

Claymont Community Center
3301 Green Street
Claymont, DE 19703

FLORIDA

Miami Area

Contact number: (305) 493-8686

Women's Resource & Counseling
  Center
(305) 448-8325
1108 Ponce de Leon Boulevard
Coral Gables, FL 33134

GEORGIA

Atlanta

Benita Esposito (404) 993-1722

HAWAII

Honolulu

Diane Sebring (808) 455-8233
1314 S. King Street, Suite 1553
Honolulu, HI 96814

IDAHO

Boise

YWCA—Dr. Glenda Loomis
(208) 343-3688
720 W. Washington
Boise, ID 83702

ILLINOIS

Chicago

Ravenswood Community
   Mental Health Center
(312) 878-7814 X1455
4545 N. Damen Avenue
Chicago, IL 60625

IOWA

Bettendorf

Family Services (319) 359-8216
Bettendorf Bank Building, Suite 220
Duck Creek Plaza
Bettendorf, IA 52722

KANSAS

Topeka Area

Family Care Center of Overland Park
(913) 648-4900
10550 Barkley, Suite 100
Overland Park, KS 66212

KENTUCKY

Ft. Thomas

National Pastoral Counseling Institute
(606) 781-1344
40 N. Grand, Suite 304
Ft. Thomas, KY 41075

LOUISIANA

Baton Rouge

Gloria Bockrath (504) 925-6922
Center for Displaced Homemakers
7393 Florida Boulevard
Baton Rouge, LA 70806

New Orleans Area

Jo Ellen Smith Psychiatric Hospital
(504) 364-3000
4601 Patterson Road
New Orleans, LA 70131

Eastlake Hospital CPC
(504) 246-2790
5650 Read Boulevard
New Orleans, LA 70127

New Life Center
(504) 899-8282 X433
De Paul Hospital
1040 Calhoun Street
New Orleans, LA 70118

Lakeside Women's Hospital
(504) 885-3333
4700 S. I-10 Service Road West
Metairie, LA 70001

MAINE

Eliot

Dr. Anne Schoonmaker
(207) 439-3306
Sunrise House
183 Main
Eliot, ME 03903

MASSACHUSETTS

Watertown

Fran Meline (617) 924-4133
131 Coolidge Avenue
Watertown, MA 02172

MINNESOTA

Minneapolis Area

Women's Resource Center
(612) 831-1144
Normandale Community College
9700 French Avenue South
Bloomington, MN 55431

St. Paul

Sara McCormack (612) 731-6364

MISSISSIPPI

Jackson

Bernie Silberman (601) 939-9030
Charter Hospital
East Lakeland Drive
Jackson, MS 39216

MISSOURI

St. Louis Area

Webster Grove Christian Church
(314) 961-3232
1320 W. Lockwood, Room 210
Webster Grove, MO 63119

Care Unit Hospital (314) 771-0500
1755 S. Grand Boulevard, Room 7-D
St. Louis, MO 63104

MONTANA

Billings

Mental Health Center (406) 252-5658
1245 N. 29th Street
Billings, MT 59103

NEBRASKA

Lincoln

Family Services (402) 471-7929
1133 'H' Street
Lincoln, NE 68508

YWCA—Kathy Kushner
(402) 476-2802
1432 'N' Street
Lincoln, NE 68508

Dr. Janet Waage Lingren
(402) 477-4500
1825 S. 77th Street
Lincoln, NE 68506
Or:

The Gathering Place (402) 488-1916
1448 'E' Street
Lincoln, NE 68508

Mij Laging (402) 475-9098
Harris House
1630 'K' Street
Lincoln, NE 68508

Southeast Community College
(402) 471-3333
8800 'O' Street
Lincoln, NE 68520

NEVADA

Las Vegas

Las Vegas Mental Health
(702) 486-6000
6161 W. Charleston
Las Vegas, NV 89102

Reno

Marilyn Shirey, MSW (702) 329-0623
Family Counseling of Northern
   Nevada
777 Sinclair Street
Reno, NV 89501

NEW HAMPSHIRE

Concord

Carol Moore (603) 228-0781
30 S. Main
Concord, NH 03301

Kathleen Klun (603) 225-2985
Womankind Counseling Center
15 Warren Street
Concord, NH 03301

Portsmouth

Women's Resource Center
(603) 436-4107
One Junkins Avenue
Portsmouth, NH 03801

NEW JERSEY

Ramsey

Contact number: (201) 825-7751

Bridgewater

New Jersey Self-Help Clearing House
(800) 367-6274
Somerset County Library, Preview
  Room
North Bridge Street
Bridgewater, NJ 08807

Camden Area

Lucy (609) 342-8208
Holy Maternity Church
431 Nickelson Road
Audubon, NJ 08106

Lawrenceville

Beverly (609) 683-7825 (home)
Lawrence Township Public Library
Route 1 Darrah Lane
Lawrenceville, NJ 08648

NEW MEXICO

Albuquerque

Maggie Moody (505) 294-7289
Center for Positive Living
8421 Osuna NE
Albuquerque, NM 87111

Pat Walke (505) 986-1718
157-O Calle Ojo Feliz
Santa Fe, NM 87505

NEW YORK

New York City

The Church of Gethsemane
(718) 499-6704
1012 8th Avenue (between 10th
  & 11th)
New York, NY 10026

St. Luke's Alcohol Center
(212) 678-6333
324 W. 108th Street
New York, NY 10025

St. Francis Bookshop (212) 736-8500
135 W. 31st Street
New York, NY 10001

COA Foundation (212) 351-2680

Tuckahoe

Ceecee (914) 632-7414
Tuckahoe Community Center
Columbus Avenue
Tuckahoe, NY 10707

NORTH CAROLINA

Greensboro

YWCA—Jimmie Gravely
(919) 273-3461
314 N. Davie Street
Greensboro, NC 27401

Raleigh

The Women's Center (919) 755-6840
315 E. Jones Street
Raleigh, NC 27601

NORTH DAKOTA

Bismarck

Lord of Life Church (701) 223-3566
1143 N. 26th Street
Bismarck, ND 58501

OHIO

Cincinnati Area

Nancy (513) 561-5695
Star Bank Building
6940 Madisonville Road
Mariemont, OH 45227

United Way Information & Referral
(513) 721-7900
Patricia Hiett-Cogan, Director

Aring Institute
6881 Beechmont Avenue
Cincinnati, OH 45230

Clermont Counseling Service
2291 Bauer Road
Batavia, OH 45103

Discovery Center
1700 Madison Road
Cincinnati, OH 45208

Mental Health Services North
  Central
7710 Reading Road
Cincinnati, OH 45237

Helen Magers, Director
(513) 381-5610
Women Helping Women
216 E. 9th Street
Cincinnati, OH 45202

Cleveland

YWCA (216) 521-8400
16915 Detroit Avenue
Lakewood, OH 44107

OREGON

Portland

Women's Health & Lifeworks
(503) 249-6636
10373 N.E. Hancock Street, Suite 115
Portland, OR 97220

Call for information on a wide range
of support groups: (503) 239-2322

Additional contact numbers:
(503) 230-0245 / (503) 657-3500

PENNSYLVANIA

Pittsburgh

Oakland Women's Center
(412) 648-2580
3802 Forbes Avenue
Pittsburgh, PA 15213

Penns Hills (412) 793-8805
Zion Lutheran Church
11609 Frankstown Road
Pittsburgh, PA 15235

Glenda Moser (412) 244-9392
5829 Ellsworth Avenue
Pittsburgh, PA 15232

SOUTH CAROLINA

Columbia

Family Service Center
(803) 733-5450
1800 Main Street
Box 7876
Columbia, SC 29202

SOUTH DAKOTA

Rapid City

Mary Baumgartner (605) 348-2677
Institute of Humanities
Magic Canyon Road
Rapid City, SD 57702

TENNESSEE

Knoxville

Rebecca Judy, LCSW
(615) 690-6326
224 Peters Road
Knoxville, TN 37923

Maryville

Kay Lloyd, PE (615) 984-9081
1944 E. Alexander Lamar Parkway
Maryville, TN 37801

TEXAS

Dallas Area

Women's Center in Richardson
(214) 238-9516
515 Custer Road
Richardson, TX 75080

Fort Worth Area

Community Service Clinic
(817) 273-2165
Graduate School of Social Work
University of Texas
Arlington, TX 76019

VERMONT

Enosburg

Enosburg Library
(802) 933-2362
Main Street
Enosburg, VT 05450

Enosburg Falls

Richford Health Center
(802) 933-2362
Main Street
Enosburg Falls, VT 05476

St. Alban's

The Family Center
(802) 524-6574
86 N. Main Street
St. Alban's, VT 05476

VIRGINIA

Petersburg

The Crater Family Counseling Service
(804) 732-3030
3277 S. Crater Road
Petersburg, VA 23803

WASHINGTON

Seattle

Contact number: (206) 367-6900 (days)
(206) 784-9476 (eves)

Women's Center (206) 546-4606
Shoreline Community College
16101 Greenwood Avenue North
Seattle, WA 98133

Bonnie Olson, MA (206) 365-3562
4218 Roosevelt Way NE
Seattle, WA 98105

Center for Christian Feminist
    Ministries
(206) 547-3374
4135 Bagley Avenue North
Seattle, WA 98103

The Learning Annex (206) 624-8900
523 Pine Street, Suite 201
Seattle, WA 98101

Judith Self (206) 823-9710

Women's Resource Center
(206) 641-2279
Bellevue Community College
3000 Landerholm Circle
Bellevue, WA 98007-6484

WEST VIRGINIA

Charleston

Women's Counseling Center
(304) 342-3724
1325-½ Summit Drive
Charleston, WV 25302

WISCONSIN

Milwaukee

Counseling Center of Milwaukee
(414) 271-2565
2038 N. Bartlett Avenue
Milwaukee, WI 53202

Women's Crisis Center (414) 937-5463
200 W. Kilbourn Avenue
Milwaukee, WI 53233

A Specialized Resource List

Because certain sources may be most helpful to you at particular stages of your recovery, the following resource list has been divided into several categories.

For the Reader in Crisis

Colgrove, Melba, M.D., Harold Bloomfield, Ph.D., and Peter A. McWilliams. *How to Survive the Loss of a Love.* New York: Bantam, 1967.

Halpern, Howard, Ph.D. *How to Break Your Addiction to a Person.* New York: McGraw-Hill, 1982.

For Sexual Addiction or Withdrawal

Augustine Fellowship. *Sex and Love Addicts Anonymous.* Boston: Fellowship-Wide Service, Inc., 1986.

For Releasing Patterns of Codependence

Beattie, Melody. *Codependent No More.* Center City, Minn.: Hazelden, 1987.

Norwood, Robin. *Women Who Love Too Much.* Los Angeles: Jeremy P. Tarcher, Inc., 1985.

Peele, Stanton, Ph.D., and Archie Brodsky. *Love and Addiction.* New York: New American Library, 1975.

For Loving Detachment

Edens, Cooper. *If You're Afraid of the Dark, Remember the Night Rainbow.* San Diego: Green Tiger Press, 1979.

Ferrucci, Piero. *What We May Be.* Los Angeles: Jeremy P. Tarcher, Inc., 1982.

For Your Inner Child

Briggs, Dorothy Corkille. *Your Child's Self-Esteem.* New York: Doubleday and Co., 1970.

Zimmerman, Bill. *Make Beliefs.* New York: Guarionex Press, 1987.

For Developing Self-Love

Lerner, Rokelle. *Daily Affirmations for Adult Children of Alcoholics.* Pompano Beach, Fla.: Health Communications, Inc., 1985.

Rubin, Theodore Isaac, M.D. *Compassion and Self-Hate.* New York: Collier Books/Macmillan, 1975.

Stoddard, Alexandra. *Living a Beautiful Life: 500 Ways to Add Elegance, Order, Beauty, and Joy to Every Day of Your Life.* New York: Random House, 1986.

For Releasing Buried Feelings

Gendlin, Eugene T., Ph.D. *Focusing.* New York: Bantam, 1978.

Miller, Alice. *The Drama of the Gifted Child.* New York: Basic Books, 1981.

For Releasing the Past

Black, Claudia, Ph.D. *Repeat after Me.* Denver, Colo.: Printing & Publications, 1985.

Leonard, Linda Schierse. *The Wounded Woman.* Athens, Ohio: Swallow Press, 1982.

For Developing Wholeness

Andrews, Lynn V. *Jaguar Woman and the Wisdom of the Butterfly Tree.* San Francisco: Harper & Row, 1985.

Ferrucci, Piero. *What We May Be.* Los Angeles: Jeremy P. Tarcher, Inc., 1982.

Koller, Alice. *An Unknown Woman.* New York: Simon & Schuster, 1982.

Small, Jacquelyn. *Transformers.* Marina del Rey, Calif.: DeVorss and Company, 1982.

For Developing Spirituality

Jung, C. G. *Memories, Dreams, Reflections.* New York: Vintage Books, 1961.

The Twelve Steps: A Way Out, Friends in Recovery, San Diego, Calif.: Recovery Publications, 1987.

For Boundary Issues

Bradshaw, John, Ph.D. *Building Boundaries.* Audiotape. Houston, Tex.: Center for Recovering Families, 1988.

Forward, Susan, Ph.D., and Joan Torres. *Men Who Hate Women and the Women Who Love Them.* New York: Bantam, 1986.

Phelps, Stanlee, and Nancy Austin. *The Assertive Woman.* Fredericksburg, Va.: Impact, 1975.

For Making New Choices

Wegscheider-Cruse, Sharon. *Choice Making.* Pompano Beach, Fla.: Health Communications, Inc., 1985.

For Releasing Yourself from a Family Role

Perera, Sylvia Brinton. *The Scapegoat Complex.* Toronto: Inner City Books, 1986.

Wegscheider, Sharon. *Another Chance.* Pompano Beach, Fla.: Health Communications, Inc., 1981.

For Increasing Your Capacity for Intimacy

Fromm, Erich, Ph.D. *The Ability to Love.* New York: Harper & Row, 1956.

Geringer-Woititz, Janet, Ed.D. *Struggle for Intimacy.* Pompano Beach, Fla.: Health Communications, Inc., 1985.

Gorski, Terence, M.A., C.A.C. *Intimacy.* Audiotape of lecture presented at ACA Convention, San Diego, Calif., January 1987. Minneapolis, Minn.: CompCare.

For Increasing Self-Esteem

Sanford, Linda Tschirhart, and Mary Ellen Donovan. *Women and Self-Esteem.* New York: Penguin Books, 1985.